Budgeting Basics:
A How-to Guide for Managers

By Allen Sweeny and John N. Wisner, Jr.

amacom
A division of American Management Associations

This book originally appeared in series form in SUPERVISORY MANAGEMENT, a monthly periodical published by AMACOM.

Cover design and art by Carol DeMauro.

International standard book number: 0-8144-6947-7.

Contents

About the Authors

Allen Sweeny is controller-treasurer of Standard Brands Incorporated.

John N. Wisner, Jr. is director of marketing services—international, Lorillard.

Preface

This book is for people in business or industry who are—or who hope to become—responsible for the planning and the activity of a specific part of their company, where this responsibility is outlined and confirmed by the existence of a budget. It is not primarily for those in the financial and accounting end of the company, though it can be useful in helping them explain what they do and why to those in the operating departments of the corporation. In short, this book is designed to explain what budgets are, how they work, and how to go about preparing and presenting them.

We addressed the book to present and future managers in nonfinancial areas. But because we give the reader full credit for his intelligence and motivation, we didn't hesitate to dig into complex or sophisticated areas—as long as we had clearly covered every basic step along the way.

We also recognized that managers look at "budgets" in a different way from that of people in the financial area. To a manager, the numbers in his budget are not cold figures—they have a personal meaning. Each unit figure, dollar amount, and percentage variance can bring to mind a problem, opportunity, or challenge he has encountered or must surmount; each has a relation to his personal and professional commitment to a planned objective.

In a book of this nature, it would be more confusing than helpful to cover every possible type or format of budget or performance comparison report. Instead, we concentrated on theory and basics—and, since we showed how these are used in practice, we believe the reader will find any format or type of budget readily understandable.

We acknowledge the assistance and understanding of a number of people who helped make this book a reality. We thank our friends at AMACOM for their help in keeping our syntax straight; their "variances" to our text were favorable. We thank our families for their forbearance; not all those weekends were rainy when Dad had a deadline and missed the fun while stuck indoors writing. We owe a large debt to all those people with whom we have worked throughout our careers and from whom we learned about budgets. And we have a special vote of thanks to Misses A. B. Ruscick and E. Tannenbaum, who turned a large collection of scribbled yellow pages and struck-over typescript into a neat, legible, and professional manuscript.

Allen Sweeny
John N. Wisner, Jr.

Chapter 1.

The purposes and uses of a budget

This morning, Joe's first as a line supervisor, was a day he'd been working toward for years. And Joe knew they had been worth it: the years of college leading to the degree; the interviewing by several companies; the decision on which company to go with; and then that strange first day at work—spent mainly in filling out innumerable forms. After that were months of the training program, during which he learned to operate various machines. He remembered all the people he had worked for; last year, he'd been one of two assistants to the supervisor in charge of producing the company's key product. All this, then, had led to the offer to take over supervision of the cough-drop line.

Joe walked from the parking lot toward the office of the plant manager, who was going to take him around to introduce him formally—both to the other supervisors he'd be working with and to the people he'd be supervising. As he walked, he reviewed what he knew about the cough-drop department.

The cough-drop line, which had been launched only two or so years ago, was a departure from the company's usual line of candy and confectionary products. But it had proven quite successful in the market place: Sales had done a good job of getting it into trade channels new to them; advertising had been good, too. The result was a whole new manufacturing line—working at just about capacity on one shift, from what he'd heard.

Although Joe had known Mr. Spencer, the plant manager, for some time, their contact had been slight. He had taken some questions to him over the past few months and, of course, he'd seen Mr. Spencer doing his daily spot-check on plant activities. But that handshake just now signalled the start of a new relationship between them. From today on, Mr. Spencer would be looking to him for anything and everything having to do with cough drops.

Later, Mr. Spencer formally introduced him not only to the people who'd be looking to him for direction, but also to those in quality control who'd be checking up on his cough drops and those in raw-materials and finished-goods warehousing who'd be sending supplies to his department and receiving the finished product from him.

SUGGESTION

As you read this series on budgeting, you may find it helpful to refer to a budget developed in your own company. (Budgeting varies from company to company and even from division to division within a single company.) Ask for—or retrieve from the files—a budget performance report for the responsibility center in which you're involved.

Finally, he had a chance to sit down at his desk in his glass-enclosed office just off the production line. There, taped to the wall, was the production schedule for the month, detailing what had to be produced by when. In the top drawer of the desk were some folders. One held copies of receipts for materials delivered: sugar, flavorings, the medicinal ingredients, packaging materials, etc. Another held copies of finished-goods receipts from the warehouse—these in shipping-case units by type or flavor.

But it was a third folder that really caught his eye. It was of a different size, designed to hold computer print-out sheets, and it was quite slim, appearing to hold only four or five pages. The label read simply, "Budgets."

He opened it and examined the top page. After a few moments it began to make sense. The heading was clear: Monthly Budget/Performance Comparison Report—Cough Drops. It was for May, the preceding month. The Budget and Actual performance columns on the left-hand side were for the month of May; a similar set of columns on the right were headed, "5 Months—Year to Date." The bottom two lines—"Total Cost" and "Total Units"—looked especially important.

Looking further, he saw that the various raw materials were expressed in pounds, quarts, and dollars. Running his eye down one of the columns he saw that "Total Cost" was the sum of all dollar amounts above it in that same column.

The budget—management tool

Most supervisors, managers, and executives in business and industry today have lived through an experience similar to Joe's. Indeed, one sign that confirms your rise to a position of real managerial responsibility is that a budget exists for the segment of company activity you will be supervising.

A budget is the key part of the entire planning and control system—a system with built-in feedback that permits management to monitor, control, and direct activities of an organization. In other words, a budget enables the management of an organization to plan for and keep close tabs on the amount of profit it makes.

Essentially, a budget is a plan for the short-term future (generally one year) expressed in numbers: numbers of dollars as well as numbers of gallons, pounds, barrels, or finished units. It is a statement of intention to act over a definite period of time—and it is agreed to by the people involved before the budgeting period starts.

The cough-drop-line production budget that Joe found in his desk was a plan that said, "We intend to produce X number of packages at a total cost of Y during the fiscal year." But this budget was not the only one having to do with cough drops. The sales department had a budget that said, "We intend to sell X number of cough-drop packages to wholesalers and retailers at a list price of W to generate Z dollars during the fiscal year." Other managers in areas such as advertising and promotion also had budgets numerically stating their intentions and established aims for cough drops.

Though Joe doesn't have to know the complete plans for cough drops for the coming year, he knows in general terms that if he doesn't perform up to budget levels, shipping won't have enough cough drops to fill the orders that sales has obtained; and if the product isn't in the stores, the advertising budget will be wasted. What Joe must know thoroughly is *his* budget—that part of the total for which he is responsible. It is his commitment as a supervisor.

Basic budget control: action versus intention

A budget says "We intend to" or "We shall." At the end of the indicated time period, the obvious question arises: "Did we?" Bookkeepers have long been needed to keep track of activity. Their reports and journals record the answers to "What did we do?" But when the bookkeeper factually states, "Sales were a million last year," the manager can go further—he can make an evaluation: "That's good. Our budget was 900 thousand."

These intentions, actions, and judgments can be pinned down and listed numerically on one line on a simple report. See Exhibit 1, page 10, for three examples.

Monthly progress reports

A company's intentions, as expressed in budgets, are for a period of time that is generally 12 months long, or a fiscal year. Usually, a fiscal year is the same as a calendar year, running from January 1 through December 31.

In the case of some small companies whose activities involve the manufacture, sale, or purchase of a limited number of big-ticket items, only one budget-against-performance comparison over one twelve-month period may be needed. But most companies want their managers and supervisors to measure their progress toward committed goals at more frequent intervals. Most companies have a monthly reporting system, although some reports on progress against budget may be issued quarterly and others may be prepared weekly.

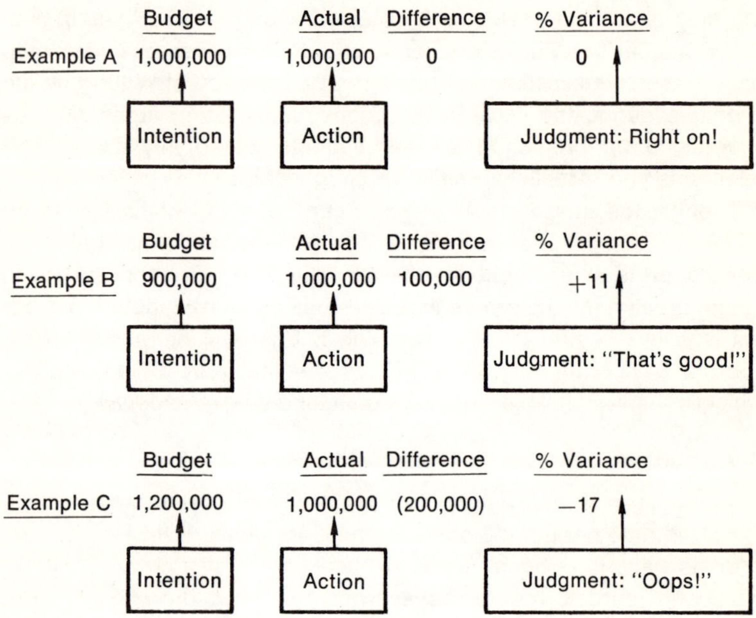

Exhibit 1.

A periodic progress report answers the question, "How are we doing in terms of our goal for the year?" Actual performance compared with budget both shows how and gives management time to correct unfavorable progress or reinforce favorable activity to ensure attainment of the budgeted goals for the year.

At the six-month mark, for instance, results to date of one half the yearly budget could indicate on-target performance. That is, if the yearly budget calls for production of 120 units, then results of 60 units at the half-year mark could seem reassuring. Unfortunately, such reassurance might be premature in most cases in business and industry. Why? Because within one twelve-month period, a series of peaks and valleys or repeating patterns may arise. These annual cycles—which are often referred to as *seasonality*—may occur in consumption, demand, and raw-material availability, to name only three. What causes these cycles? For one thing, a number of products and services are climate-oriented: cough drops in winter and sunglasses in summer, for example.

The seasonality patterns of other companies may follow calendar events. Greeting-card companies are good examples. They promote such calendar-oriented celebrations as Easter, Valentine's Day, Thanksgiving, and Christmas. But consumer demand for their products is heaviest for Christmas cards. You and I and millions of others don't start thinking about Christmas cards until around Thanksgiving, and rarely before Hallowe'en. Sales of Christmas cards thus peak to consumers in November and December. Sales to retail stores peak in October and November, as do shipments from the manufacturer.

Say that the Best Wish Card Company makes a complete line of greeting cards, and that half their yearly dollar volume comes from Christmas cards. If they sell $12 million worth of cards in a year, then $6 million come from Christmas cards and all $6 million will hit their books over the two-month period of October and November. No workable fiscal year can be constructed that will put 50 percent of their sales in each of two six-month periods.

Let's assume a year that coincides with the calendar year. Let's also say that their general line of greeting cards sells evenly throughout the year. Their sales pattern, by quarter, will look like this:

	Jan/Mar	*Apr/Jun*	*Jul/Sep*	*Oct/Dec*
Greeting Cards	25%	25%	25%	25%
Christmas Cards	—	—	—	100%

Assuming similar selling prices, their dollar sales will thus take the following pattern:

	Jan/Mar	*Apr/Jun*	*Jul/Sep*	*Oct/Dec*
$ Sales	12.5%	12.5%	12.5%	62.5%

Their yearly production pattern will be similar, but will peak one quarter earlier:

	Jan/Mar	*Apr/Jun*	*Jul/Sep*	*Oct/Dec*
Unit Production	12.5%	12.5%	62.5%	12.5%

And their raw material purchases will naturally peak even earlier.

If the purchasing, production, sales, shipping, and finance departments at Best Wish Card Company don't take these patterns into account in preparing monthly breakdowns of their yearly budgets, a serious lack of activity control will result.

Trends versus annual cycles

Let's look at another factor that will normally have to be taken into account in breaking a yearly budget down into shorter time periods. This is the actual or planned trend, which is normally upward.

For this purpose, let's look at sales of widgets, the only product we know that has absolutely no seasonality in demand throughout the year—since for our purposes here, this is how we have defined the demand for it. Let us say that the sales of these widgets are growing 20 percent per year. Last year, 83 zillion were sold; this year, 100 zillion will be sold—so it's obvious that we should budget for sales of 120 zillion next year.

How, then, should we break sales of 120 zillion widgets down into months? The quick—and incorrect—answer is 10 zillion per month. It's incorrect because it ignores the rising, incremental trend in demand during the year, and states that the incremental increase in demand will jump once in the year, during the very first month, and remain constant over the next 11 months. What will actually happen is that monthly sales at the beginning of the year will be about 8.6 zillion per month, and monthly sales at the end of the year will be about 11.4 zillion per month. The monthly pattern over the year, of course, will be a straight line that slopes upward.

Interim performance measurement

The cycle and trend of actual results will thus be among the factors that help us determine whether results to date are good or bad. If the yearly budget is 70 zillion, and if results at the six-month mark are 35 zillion, then the target is 50 percent achieved in 50 percent of the time. But the evaluation, "We're on target," can be made only if the budget, as broken down by months, indicates that the intention was to be at the 50 percent level after 6 months.

Great care must be taken in breaking budgets down into the same number of time periods during which results will be reported. A discussion of this and a worksheet method will be found in a later section on budget preparation.

Though the actual results to date and the planned results to date are important, for management purposes the key number (and most useful fact) is their *difference*. To illustrate, let's look at the bottom two lines on the 5-month Performance Report that Joe found in his new desk.

	May		5 Months—Year to Date			
	Budget	*Actual*	*Budget*	*Actual*	*Diff.*	%
Total Cost	$3,000	$3,500	$33,000	$36,630	$3,630	+11
Total Units Produced	100,000	120,000	1,100,000	1,256,000	156,000	+14

For both the month of May and the five months to date, total cost has exceeded budget. Costs to date stand 11 percent over budget, which normally is not a good situation. The explanation, however, is in the next line: Total units produced have, in the same period, exceeded the unit budget by 156,000—a 14 percent difference over budget. This obviously is a good turn of events.

Thus, in the five months to date, units produced are 14 percent ahead of the budgeted goal. The costs incurred to produce these units are only 11 percent over budget—so this variance, which at first looked unfavorable, is highly favorable in proper perspective.

But how can unit production and the cost of production have different variances? After all, one is a function of the other. One answer is that the budget for each was established by different people who were working with different assumptions. Happily, this kind of error occurs only rarely today. Why? Because managers today have a better understanding of the need for overall coordination in the budgeting process. The answer is much more likely to be found in an analysis of the components of the total cost. Accountants normally charge to each budget center a share of the total fixed costs incurred by the total facility—administrative expenses, rent or building depreciation, janitorial service, and so forth. They also charge the budget center with depreciation for the machinery used by this center, and a machine will depreciate a fixed amount per time period regardless of its use. Because they are fixed (or period) costs, none of those costs vary with volume of production. However, variable (or direct) costs such as raw materials, packaging materials, and labor increase and decrease with production volume and will, therefore, normally have the same variances from budget as unit production.

So it's easy to see that fixed costs per unit would drop as unit production increases, but increase as the number of units drop. Variable (direct) costs per unit, however, would go up or down at the same rate as a rise or drop in production. When unit production exceeds the budgeted figure, therefore, only the variable components of total production cost increase—so total production cost obviously increases at a lesser rate than units produced.

In examining budget reports, managers soon learn to skim quickly down the variance column. The essence of the report is the total variance, which in turn is the total of all the variances for each part of this total. The eye quickly finds the big positive or negative variances, and the mind quickly determines whether they are favorable or unfavorable and how important they are.

At higher management levels, budget reports can be lengthy. The eye can quickly get lost in a sea of numbers, and a key variance—whether favorable or unfavorable—might be missed. In cases like these, management says, "Don't tell me where we're on target or only slightly off; that's for the line supervisor or unit manager. Just show me the items that are more than (say) 10 percent ahead of or behind budget." This procedure results in a much shorter report that highlights both opportunities and problems. These abridged reports are generally called "exception reports."

Budgets—philosophy and uses

A manager does more than just supervise the work of others—he also plans the work. The plan he follows, distilled into numbers, is his budget. The report comparing his actual results with his projected budget results (specifically, the variances between these) reveals the progress he is making toward his goal.

In the development, discussion, and presentation of a budget, the following topics must be taken up during the planning process:

1. *Organization.* Are we properly organized for the job of reaching the target?
2. *Delegation.* Are the key pieces of the job properly delegated to people who understand the importance of their individual segments?
3. *Priorities.* Have the few key elements, tasks, or interim goals been identified in terms both of importance and of the order in which they must be achieved?
4. *Resources.* Have the available resources (facilities, machinery, raw materials, etc.) been properly allocated in terms of the target and the priorities involved?

Joe may not formulate these topics so precisely when he's putting together next year's budget for the cough-drop line. They may only cross his mind. But for Joe's boss, the plant manager—and for *his* boss, the division manager—these are very real concerns.

Joe will not receive formal approval of his budget until the plant manager hears from the division manager that he has received the go-ahead from corporate management. During each successive budget presentation and review stage, the budget process will: (1) identify opportunities, (2) define problems, (3) aid decision making, and (4) help coordinate efforts. And once approval is given down the line, the budget process automatically will (5) provide performance measures.

Budget comparison reports

Let's say that the budget is approved, performance measures have been established, and the fiscal year is under way. Periodically, reports comparing actual results versus performance targets are issued, and variances from plan are revealed. These variances will stimulate the same kind of managerial considerations that arise during the budget review process, since they, too, will: (1) identify opportunities, (2) define problems, (3) aid decision making, and (4) help coordinate efforts.

If important opportunities or problems are revealed by progress reports, managers up and down the ladder will want to take steps to ensure that the basic target will be met or exceeded. The first step will be to re-examine—in view of performance to date—the four main parts of the planning process: (1) organization, (2) delegation, (3) priorities, and (4) resource allocation.

Importance to the individual supervisor

The concientious manager committed to his responsibilities and goals wants to know from time to time the answer to a very human question: "How am I doing?" The monthly progress reports will tell him and will also tell all those who see a copy of each report. How he uses the information in each report and the trend of his variances over a series of reports will tell his superiors even more about what kind of manager he is.

Upon receiving a report showing important variances, the smart manager will analyze the situation for himself. He will recognize that a variance results from either the budget side (planning) or the results side. He will analyze whether the budget was over- or underoptimistic; he will investigate whether the problems encountered or the opportunities exploited led to the actual results for the period. The next wise step is to review this analysis with his superior. If it's an important analysis, it should be submitted in writing—along with a statement of corrective or reinforcing measures being taken. Some companies ask their managers for this kind of write-up in the form of monthly management reports.

Of greater personal importance to the individual manager, however, is the budget preparation and presentation stage. This is his opportunity to formulate new programs and propose new actions. A key responsibility of each manager is to plan—and budget-presentation time provides him with a once-a-year opportunity to show how well he can plan, how creative (and how practical) he is.

The yearly budget presentation is also important to the individual supervisor or manager because usually it allows him to demonstrate ability and knowledge—not only to the immediate boss, but often to top management as well. Pushing for acceptance of the proposed budget—or, conversely, defending it—is easier when the budget/performance measurement system is clearly understood. ■

Chapter 2.

Budget control through responsibility centers

The immortal coach, Vince Lombardi, said, "Winning isn't the only thing; it's everything." For business, it's much the same: Profits aren't the only thing; they're everything. Earlier, we discussed budgeting as a managerial tool used in planning and tracking an organization's profits. Now let's look at the structural decentralization of budget control into "responsibility" centers within an organization—a necessary development in large, complex companies. These centers break the organization down into smaller, more manageable components—each headed by a manager who has accepted responsibility for budget control of his segment and who has the authority to make decisions within it.

Basically, a responsibility center is a segment of a business to which a series of organizational and accounting controls are applied to evaluate how effectively the manager of the unit is carrying out the responsibility delegated to him. There are several kinds of responsibility centers—each with its uses and limitations.

The revenue center

The first form of responsibility center, the "revenue center," simply delegates to a section of the organization the responsibility for generating sales. Revenue centers, which have been well established in American industry for years, are probably most familiar in terms of the annual "sales budget." Under the revenue concept, the responsibility for generating a certain level of revenue is delegated to an appropriate part of the organization. That level usually takes the form of a "budget," or target, against which actual performance is compared. Usually, progress is also presented against last year's performance.

The cost center

The "cost center" concept is probably even more familiar than the revenue center. Almost all private and public institutions now have some form of cost-center approach to organization. Under this approach, each group within the organization is responsible for controlling the costs it incurs in carrying out organizational responsibilities. The cost-center approach to organization usually begins with the preparation of a cost budget that sets forth a proposed or estimated level of expenses for a given time period—usually a calendar year. This budget is reviewed by top management, which may call for revisions before approving it. Once it is approved, the actual costs incurred are accounted for by the cost center. When there are unfavorable variances, management and the person responsible for the cost center himself can take corrective action. Earlier, we saw Joe involved in a classic budget under a cost center.

Limitations of revenue and cost centers

Although revenue and cost centers are widely useful, each has limitations that are, in a sense, related. On one hand, the revenue center provides management with control and measurement of revenue generation—but gives no indication of the costs being incurred to obtain the revenue. Conversely, the cost center provides management with a tool for controlling costs as budgeted—but doesn't show the revenue or benefit to which these costs lead. Both the revenue and the cost-center concept fail to control or evaluate the more basic business objective—profitability.

The profit center

As a result, management turned to the development of the profit-center concept—which consists of delegating responsibility for generating revenue and controlling associated costs to yield the targeted profit level. But although the profit center has significant advantages over a revenue or cost center, it too has limitations.

A major problem concerns the balance between long-range and short-range profitability. Before we get more specific, let's digress briefly to investigate these terms. Someone once defined business as the delicate art of making decisions that are an appropriate trade-off between long- and short-term profitability. Probably no other comment goes more to the heart of top management responsibility. Any business can be "milked" for a profit—even stripped of assets in the press for profit *now.* The real challenge is to maintain an adequate level of current profitability and solvency—and *at the same time* provide growth for future profitability. In today's dynamic markets, where product life-cycles grow shorter and shorter, this task becomes even more difficult.

Getting back to the profit-center concept, a major problem is that it can often create undue pressure on a manager to achieve short-term profit objectives at the expense of the longer term health of the organization. In such a situation, a manager may ditch organizational development, new-product development, major plant expansions, and other actions that lay the base for future profitability—all in order to realize and comply with the short-term, net-income commitments of his profit center.

Congruence between profit center and organization

When profit responsibility is delegated, the manager of a decentralized profit center must obviously take actions congruent with those of the overall corporation. In practice, however, this rather simple notion is often more difficult than it would seem. Certainly, it can limit the effectiveness of the profit-center approach.

Here's a case in point. Often, a manufacturing or other company unit in one profit center will transfer its product to another company unit (another profit center)—which must pay a "purchase" price for the product before actually selling it. But because the two units have difficulty in establishing a realistic purchase price, the profit center purchaser finds little incentive to sell the product. So it will direct its advertising, promotion, and selling efforts toward a product on which it can enjoy a higher profit and thus improve its profitability. The fact may be, however, that the original unit selling the product enjoys a much higher margin. But because the purchasing profit center receives no benefit from this margin, it promotes the sale of other products—even though promoting the selling profit center's products would bring in greater profits for the total corporation.

Another case in point: A profit center disposes of some manufacturing facilities that it no longer needs in order to eliminate the associated depreciation expense (and possibly realize a profit). It may do so even though some other profit center in the company needs these facilities. These are but two of many "incongruences" that can arise between the net-income objectives of the individual profit center and those of the overall corporation.

Measures such as realistic, though unofficial, transfer prices and centralized controls for disinvestments are examples of controls designed to correct such incongruences. Even so, however, the achievement of real congruence between the activities of an individual profit center and overall corporate objectives is often difficult and should be recognized as such in administering a profit center.

Under the profit-center approach, an undue emphasis on short-term, expedient, "performance" profitability may be encouraged in other ways, too. For example, profits growing out of continual cutbacks in advertising expense will probably be obtained at the expense of a loss in "share of market." Similarly, the costs involved in the following areas may be minimized or avoided simply by doing nothing: new-product development, research, mechanization and automation, and manpower and organizational development. Again, however, the benefits to short-term profits would undoubtedly impair the profit center's base for future sales and earnings growth.

Obviously, then, net income should not be the exclusive performance yardstick. Rather, profit results should be interpreted in light of whether the actions taken also maintain and build the future of the business—in ways such as the following: growth in share of mar-

Exhibit 2: Return on investment from two profit centers

	Profit centers	
	A	B
Net Income	$100,000	$200,000
Investment	$1,000,000	$4,000,000
Return on Investment	10%	5%

ket, new-product development, organizational development, mechanization and automation of accounting and administrative systems, and plant modernization.

Profits: a relative matter

Although we have emphasized the importance of profits to a business, profits by themselves do not tell the full story. Consider, for example, two profit centers: Profit Center A earns $100,000 a year; Center B earns $200,000. Seemingly, Profit Center B is twice as profitable as Profit Center A. However, if the funds invested in Profit Center A amount to $1,000,000—compared with $4,000,000 invested in Profit Center B—we draw a different conclusion about the relative value of the two profit centers in terms of their return on investment. The reason for this different conclusion is highlighted in Exhibit 2, above. Profit Center A has twice the return on investment of Profit Center B.

The profits of a business (and/or, of course, a profit center) may be large or small. They may increase or decrease—but when all is said and done, the net income of the enterprise really tells us very little unless we know how much investment was required to generate this income. The critical consideration in assessing the *adequacy* of profits in any given situation is the return they provide in relationship to the investment required to generate them.

The relationship of net income (profits) to investment indicates the return on investment (ROI). ROI is all-important to any business, for three basic reasons:

1. As shown in Exhibit 3, p. 22, under normal circumstances growth in profit increases with an increasing return on investment.

2. Adequate return is necessary in order to sustain dividend payment and effect reinvestments.

3. As a general rule, investors seek an adequate and stable return on their investments. Therefore, it's important for a business to main-

Exhibit 3: The relationship between earnings increase and increased return on investment

EZ CORPORATION

	Year 1	Year 2	Year 3
Common Equity (Investment)	100.00	100.00	100.00
Net Income	10.00	10.50	11.02
Return on Equity (Investment)	10.0%	10.5%	11.0%
Increase in Return		5%	5%
Increase in Earnings		5%	5%

tain such a return in order to attract additional equity capital for its future investments.

All these considerations have led to the final stage in the evolution of the responsibility center concept—the return on investment center.

The return-on-investment (ROI) center

As its name suggests, the concept of the return-on-investment center involves the decentralization not only of profit responsibility, but also of responsibility for good management of the assets used to produce the profit. Knowing that the ROI center measures his effectiveness in both areas, the manager is interested not only in turning a profit, but also in effectively utilizing the assets required to produce it. A significant advantage: This approach places on the manager the same requirements that are critical to the overall corporation.

Another great appeal of the ROI approach to managerial control is the scope of factors encompassed in the final determination of such return. (See Exhibit 4, page 23.)

Limitations of the ROI center

The ROI center also has limitations, of which the major ones follow:

Fixed-Asset Valuation. Various studies have indicated that almost all companies using ROI control systems include fixed assets in the investment base, whether they are to be valued at gross (before depreciation) or net book value. (The investment base is the denominator, and profit the numerator, in the ROI ratio.)

Exhibit 4: Factors contributing to return on investment

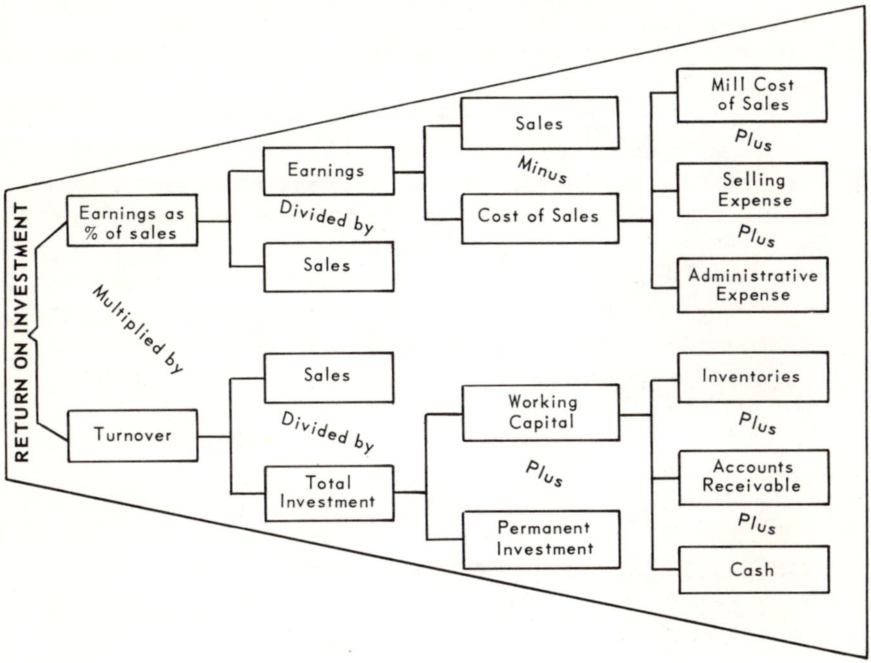

If fixed assets are valued on the basis of their gross value, there is a singular temptation for the manager to improve his ROI by disposing of a fixed asset, since the reduction will be in the gross amount, or original cost of the asset—not its depreciated value after years of use.

Fixed assets valued on the basis of net book value are also often valued according to group depreciation policies for income-tax purposes. (The IRS has set up classifications for fixed or capital assets. Allowances for depreciation are made according to the classification in which particular assets fall.) Consequently, the disposal of an asset valued on a net book basis and under group depreciation policies will not *necessarily* bring about a significant reduction in the investment denominator. This factor argues for the use of the net book value as a basis for valuation. But the use of net book value can also lead to distortions. Why? Because the simple passage of time constantly depreciates an asset and consequently reduces its net value—thus effecting increases in the return of the ROI center that are not a result of improved performance.

There is no perfect solution for valuing fixed assets—as we'll note later, it's not the valuation used that is important, but rather *how* it is used.

Further Problems in Fixed-Asset Valuation. We have already discussed some of the complications involved in deciding on whether fixed assets should be included on a gross or a net basis in the investment denominator. With either approach, the fixed assets will almost always be shown (in accordance with conventional accounting practice) at values based on their original cost. In the face of ever-increasing rates of annual inflation, the use of original costs can misrepresent the return under present or future conditions when the assets have to be replaced at their higher current values. The return of a profit center (or even of a total company, for that matter) can temporarily benefit merely from the fact that investments in fixed assets were made many years in the past.

Leased "assets" can also present a problem. Current standard accounting policies recognize that a company can generate revenues through "off balance sheet" assets in the form of leases (that is, assets used in the operation of a business, but paid for in terms of leasing expenses rather than through the depreciation of a company investment). The same advantage can exist for an ROI center within the corporation. It is entirely conceivable that ROI Center A may have a better return than ROI Center B simply because its assets are leased and therefore do not form part of the investment base—whereas those of Center A have been purchased and do form part of the base, thereby increasing the denominator and lowering the resultant ROI percentage.

"Sunk" Past Fixed-Asset Investments. One factor that makes the capital investment decision so important is the length of time (anywhere from ten to fifty years) during which it affects profitability. New marketing initiatives can be quite costly if the new products fail, but they can at least be curtailed in a relatively short period of time. Fixed-asset investments, however, are monuments to the "future"—and, once made, they are often difficult to reverse. Furthermore, the current manager of an ROI center inherits capital-investment decisions made by his predecessors; the decisions they made linger on in the form of fixed assets included in the investment base.

The depreciation expenses, as well as the investment associated with these past decisions, are "sunk." Because they are "water over the dam," the expenses and investment associated with such past decisions can be eliminated only with a strategic and costly corporate disinvestment decision. More often than not, the alternative is to "rock along" in a marginal situation and hope somehow that things will improve.

The point in all this is that profits don't always materialize as expected on every investment. In fact, return on investment varies for different businesses.

Despite all these facts, it is popularly believed that the ROI control system permits a ready comparison of one manager's performance with that of another on the basis of a single index. Business life just isn't that simple—and a major problem is that the ROI approach can tempt management to think it is.

ROI Congruence with Corporate Objectives. Since the numerator in the ROI fraction reflects profit, a profit center under ROI control will have the same problems of maintaining congruence with corporate objectives as do other kinds of responsibility centers. And, with an ROI center, there is the additional complication of assuring that the handling of asset investments is also congruent with overall corporate objectives.

Since the ROI percentage is the result of a profit numerator divided by an investment denominator, a manager can improve his performance simply by reducing the investment denominator rather than increasing the profit numerator. (Controls are needed to ensure that a manager won't succumb to the temptation to increase his ROI by disposing of assets that could be of use and value elsewhere in the corporation—or could generate adequate profits if properly managed.) Moreover, a manager may be reluctant to increase the investment denominator (and thus lower his ROI) even though doing so might, over the long term, be in the best interests of the corporation.

Short-term vs. long-term ROI

As with the profit center, the ROI center can tempt a manager to maximize short-term return at the expense of the long-term health of the business. Most major capital investments or significant development programs don't reach their full profit potential for several —or, indeed, many—years. Moreover, the start-up expenses of such major projects usually have an initial adverse effect on net income.

Unless this potential effect is recognized, and in some manner adjusted for, the ROI center approach to control can actually discourage the major long-term investments essential for future growth of the profit center.

Overcoming distortions in ROI center control

Accounting's use of the "cost concept" has long been under attack, but no one has been able to find a practical, more objective alternative. However, research for alternatives is bound to intensify —particularly in today's world of double-digit inflation.

Under the conventional cost concept, as we have seen, the performance of one ROI center can appear to be better than another only because the assets under the manager's control are older. But there are ways to correct at least some of the distortions created by accounting procedures used in ROI measurement. There are, for example, managerial accounting practices (versus financial accounting practices) that can "statistically" show fixed assets at some estimate of the current value. This modification not only reduces distortions created by use of the cost concept, but also places various ROI centers on a more realistic parity with each other.

Another way to correct the distorted picture of managerial performance that arises from marginal "sunk" investments is simply to look not only at absolute returns, but also at the trend in the return on investment. A good manager saddled with a marginal ROI center may have the lowest return in the coporation—but his record of improvement may be the best. It is this record that should be used to evaluate his performance.

Even though marketing-development costs are vital to the long-term generation of revenues, conventional accounting procedures can actually discourage the ROI manager from undertaking long-term marketing-development programs. By adopting internal management-accounting procedures that allow such costs to be amortized, a company may obtain a more accurate matching of expenses with revenues for an ROI center, and encourage sound marketing-development programs.

The residual-income concept: variation of the ROI concept

A most important adaptation of the ROI center approach is the residual income approach. Under this approach, a division is measured by its profits minus a charge for the capital it employs. Before looking at an illustration of this variation, let's look at a comparison of ROI centers based on the standard ROI concept:

	ROI centers	
	A	B
Net Income	400	1,500
Investment	2,000	10,000
ROI	20%	15%

Under this concept, ROI Center A is obviously more successful than ROI Center B. The proponents of the residual income method argue that the traditional use of the ROI ratio to determine success begs the question of whether it's better to earn a high rate of return on a small amount of capital, or a smaller, but satisfactory, return on a larger amount of capital.

The question is not academic. Suppose, for example, that the relevant cost of corporate capital applicable to ROI Centers A and B were 12 percent. Viewed in terms of the residual-income concept, their performance would appear as follows:

	ROI centers	
	A	B
Net Income	400	1,500
Less Cost (12%) on Investment Employed	240	1,200
Residual Income	160	300

Here, the judgment on which ROI center had better performance is reversed. The rationale: ROI Center B made the greater absolute contribution to profits even though it doesn't have the higher ROI ratio. But this is exactly the point espoused by those who argue for the use of the residual-income concept: Each manager must improve *absolute* dollar profits, not ratios. In addition to providing an incentive for more profitable operations to grow, the residual-income concept:

- Allows management to set an absolute goal or standard rather than try to maximize an index.
- Makes it practical to use different rates of return for different types of assets—thereby adjusting for the age of assets or the degree of risk stemming from the business in which they are employed.

• Makes it possible for similar types of assets to earn the same return regardless of the present levels of profitability—thereby facilitating a more direct comparison between the profit performance of ROI centers.

Despite these advantages, however, the residual-income method does not solve the problems of asset valuation that arise in the ROI center. Nor does it overcome the inherent difficulties of annual profits as a real gauge of managerial success. Moreover, it poses yet another, even more complicating consideration: The conclusion that Venture B is in fact more successful than Venture A depends upon the assessment of the real and relevant cost of the capital employed in each center.

Suppose, for example, that the cost of capital is considered to be 15 percent rather than 12 percent. Our assessment of the success of the two ROI centers would be quantified as follows:

	ROI centers	
	A	B
Net income	400	1,500
Less Cost (15%) on Investment Employed	300	1,500
Residual Income	100	0

As this illustration demonstrates, not even the residual-income concept can unequivocally point to the more successful ROI center. Obviously, under one assessment of the cost of capital, ROI Center A is more successful; under another assessment, Center B is. It can be argued that this distinction would be obscured altogether under a standard ROI approach, and this is true. Under any system, the only certainty is that as a managerial tool, ROI control systems can be used as an aid to—never as a substitute for—good, commonsensical business judgment. ■

Chapter 3.

Responsibility accounting

Every month, and in some companies more often, nonfinancial supervisors and managers come into contact either with accountants or with the reports they prepare. As was mentioned earlier, these reports are normally oriented toward income, expense, profit, or financial return, not toward the balance sheet and operating statement that are the concern of the accountant responsible for preparing the reports required by the federal and state government agencies and by stock exchanges. (With the federal corporate income-tax rate now at 48 percent, there is obviously a need to prepare these reports accurately.) Typical reports to managers do not merely report on results, they measure progress toward a goal. They are the individual manager's budget- or performance-comparison report, and they report on his specific area of responsibility.

Accounting keeps track

The work done in the accounting department to keep track of all the items of income and expense, as well as the budget against which these are to be compared, is called "responsibility accounting." The accounting manager who supervises this activity is usually the controller.

As we discussed last month, responsibility accounting forms the basis for an effective managerial system of planning and control; it bears only a tangential relationship to the official bookkeeping and accounting required for legal and tax reasons. For tax or other reasons, a company may be organized into several corporations, and official books are kept for each legal entity. At the same time, the same company may be organized in an entirely different way to manage its business. (In these cases, the responsibility for actually managing the business and the responsibility for maintaining legal entities do not meet except at top management levels.)

One manager—one responsibility center

Earlier in this series, we stated that one definition of a manager is that he is someone with budget responsibility—the responsibility of guiding or affecting results of the operation, department, or group he supervises toward an agreed-to goal. In short, a manager supervises a responsibility center. We also outlined earlier the number of different ways in which responsibility centers can be organized. The type of responsibility center—and the resulting planning and control system, or "budget"—developed for each manager depends on the scope of the manager's responsibility.

For a *production supervisor,* a simple cost center is adequate to measure responsibility and performance versus quantity, cost, and productivity targets—as we saw earlier with Joe and his cough-drop line.

A *regional sales manager* will most probably have his performance reported in a revenue-center format. His main responsibilities will be unit and dollar sales, with special considerations in the areas of price mix, discount mix, and possibly cost mix as well.

For a *brand or product manager,* the usual mechanism for reporting on responsibility is a simple profit center. This normally takes the form of an abbreviated income (profit and loss, or P&L) statement; it includes sales, cost of sales, and marketing expenses (advertising, sales promotion, market research). The bottom line is not profit because a number of expenses not under the brand manager's control (salaries, administrative overhead, taxes, and so forth) are not included. This bottom line, the brand manager's basic commitment, is thus called "brand contribution" or "brand profit." To see how the complexities posed by working within a profit-center format are straightened out in practice, take a look at the box on page 33.

For the *general manager of a division* or subsidiary involved in a distinct or separate activity, the use of some form of an ROI responsibility center is frequently practical. The key consideration in establishing an ROI center is the accountant's ability to separate the total investment or assets into clean, logical operational parts without having to allocate to other areas a number of costs that are not directly attributable to the responsibility center or product. Efficiencies resulting from the centralization of sales and manufacturing sometimes can rule against the establishment of practical ROI centers.

Tracking budget variances—from the bottom up

At the end of any budget reporting period, it is unusual to find any responsibility center with its key bottom line exactly on budget. There is generally a variance, however small. It is unheard-of to have every responsibility center in a company with a zero variance.

Budget variances are a fact of managerial life. The interplay between responsibility-center variances are interesting in a theoretical sense and can be extremely important in practice.

Every manager's budget variance forms a part of his boss's variance. If the cough-drop line supervisor has a $1,000 cumulative variance at the end of July, this $1,000 amount will be part of the variance through July of his boss, the production manager.

Manufacturing Cost Variances Through July	
Cough-drop production	+$1,000
Candy production	−500
Chocolate-bar production	+250
Total production variance	+$ 750

Working in Profit and ROI Centers: Theory and Practice

The profit-center approach often used with brand or product managers manifests many of the problems inherent in a profit or ROI responsibility-center approach, so let's examine the workings of this organizational arrangement more closely.

One of the basic goals in establishing a planning and control system for a manager's responsibility center is to include all the facets of the area for which he is responsible—and leave out those over which he has no direct control. At first glance, therefore, an abbreviated P&L profit-center format for a brand manager is not properly set up because it includes expenses not under his control. This condition, however, reflects a reality of structural operation. In most multibrand companies, neither the sales nor the manufacturing departments report to brand management. But in order to deliver the committed brand profit, the brand manager must be involved with both sales and manufacturing.

In practice, this theoretical contradiction is resolved at the budget-planning stage and throughout the year as well. The sales budget prepared and proposed to management is the result of discussions and agreement between the brand and sales managers; in these discussions, they agree to unit and dollar sales (by size or packing) as well as sales strategies, sales promotion and advertising objectives, and strategies designed to make the sales target achievable. During the year, the brand manager will carefully watch sales by size because a change in the expected sales mix can have important effects on profit delivered.

The brand manager will also confer with the manufacturing people at budget time and during the year. Although the brand manager does not control production, he must know both the costing formula and standard or proposed costs for his brand. If raw material or labor costs increase beyond predicted limits, he can consider reducing the part of his product's cost that he *can* control: packaging format and contents. Sometimes savings are made possible by changing packaging-material specifications or using one less color. More drastic measures to protect profit levels include a price increase or a reduction in package contents.

Production lines are generally set up as cost centers. An overbudget variance in a cost center represents an expense greater than called for by the budget—an unfavorable variance, naturally. In a revenue center, a profit center, and an ROI center, on the other hand, the overbudget variance is favorable because it means that revenue, profit, or return has gone over the budgeted figure. In a profit-center budget-comparison report, variances within the report are usually identified as favorable or unfavorable—thus avoiding the *over* and *under* terminology, and possible confusion. See Exhibit 5, below.

In the exhibit, the only line with an overbudget variance is cost of sales, which is thus unfavorable. The other items are under budget; again, all are unfavorable except advertising and promotion—where, of course, the underbudget variance is favorable.

Tracking budget variances—from the top down

A good budgeting and performance reporting system is not just for information; it is for use. A good system that provides good information to a good manager leads to action at the right place—the lowest possible level of action. A good system will also lead to action at all levels of management.

PRODUCT PROFIT CENTER

Budget Comparison Report—Through July

	Budget	Actual	Favorable	(Unfavorable)	%
	($)	($)	($)	($)	
Sales	10,000	9,200		(800)	(8.0)
Less Cost of Sales	6,000	6,100		(100)	(1.7)
Gross Profit	4,000	3,100		(900)	(22.5)
Less Advertising & Promotion	1,500	1,400	100		6.7
Product Contribution	2,500	1,700		(800)	(32.0)

Exhibit 5

At the higher management levels, managers can call on staff assistance for analysis of variances. By tracking variances from the top down, a task that is streamlined if exception reports are used, a summary of even a giant corporation's performance versus the established goals can be prepared quickly. See Exhibit 6, page **36**.

Following the numbered arrows in the exhibit down through each report, we see that:

1. The major problem area is Division A.

2. Within Division A, it is Brand 1 that is in trouble.

3. The trouble with Brand 1 is in the area of cost of goods sold.

4. Brand 1's manufacturing cost variance is highly unfavorable.

5. The large negative raw materials variance is the cause of the unfavorable manufacturing cost variance.

Obviously, Exhibit 6 was created to show how variances can be tracked all the way down the line. They were thus kept simple and abbreviated. Nevertheless, it is possible to see how a one-line item on a report to top management represents the combined efficiency of thousands of individual operations and reveals the combined performance of hundreds of individual supervisors and managers.

In going all the way down to the bottom and working back up, it is interesting to track the way in which a major $75,000 variance in the material for one product is reduced by other cost elements in the production supervisor's responsibility center. His variance is further eased at the brand contribution level by a favorable sales variance, a part of which is lost on the advertising line. The other brands in the division are closer to budget than Brand 1, so not much help is found there. One step up, Division B shows a nice favorable variance in contrast to Division C's shortfall, and the total company's profit variance is thus helped some more.

The above analysis shows just one of the literally hundreds of variance pathways that can be followed from the top down to the bottom. This one traced its way from major variance to major variance. The experienced analyst will not stop here, however. To satisfy his curiosity and discharge his responsibility, he'll want to dig behind the variances reported for the other divisions as well. Historical performance information will prompt him to take another look at Brand 3, which in previous reports has been showing even greater favorable variances. And for Brand 1, how was the $16,000 variance in packaging materials obtained?

One more dimension is added to variance analysis in its application in real life today: time. Two analyses of variances done one

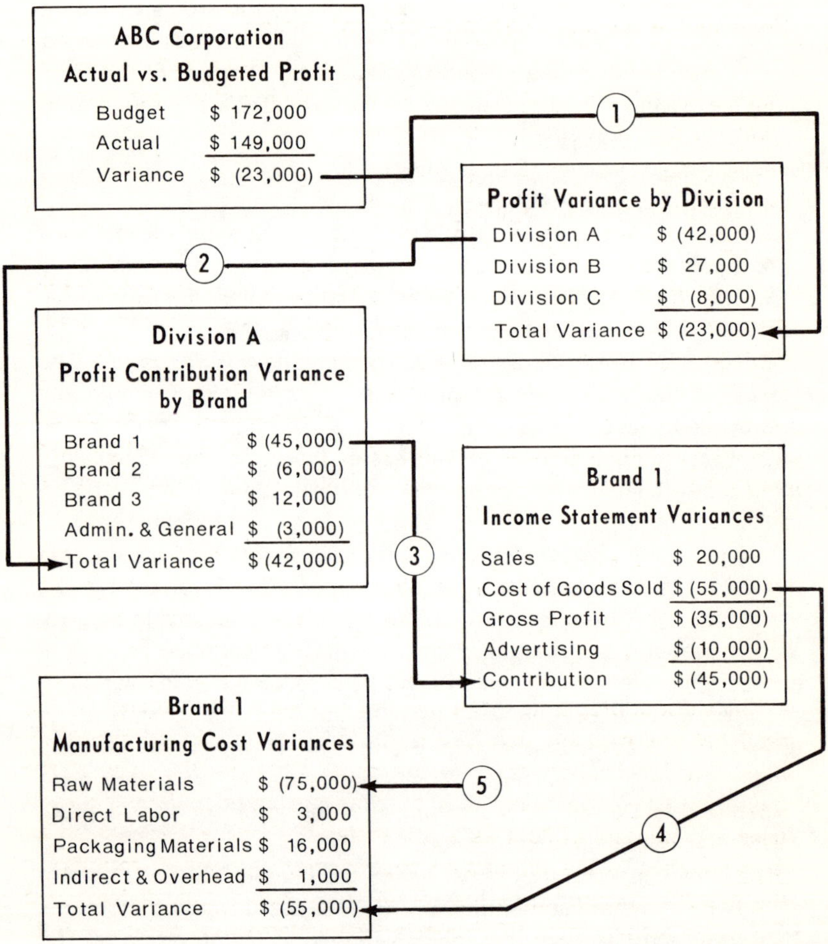

Exhibit 6

month apart show how the variances are varying. More than two will help the analyst—and the manager—determine whether a trend has been established. And if a trend is suspected, deeper examination is required to dig out the reasons and the factors at work. Every manager wants to correct a problem or exploit an opportunity as soon as possible.

Keeping the numbers straight—account coding

The accountants in a company have the job of keeping the books and issuing all the various responsibility-center reports for management. To be useful, each of these reports must be:

1. *Complete.* The omission of one or more items can lead to an incorrect total; the manager who believes and uses it can make a wrong decision and take unwise or disastrous action.

2. *Accurate.* Though only addition and subtraction are required for most reports, the pressure of time can lead to an embarrassing mistake. Classic goofs can creep into manually prepared reports when numbers are transposed (an *85* gets copied as *58*) or entered in the wrong line on the report. These errors can sometimes get by the accountant's double-checks; the manager should thus question numbers on his reports that don't "look" right or fit the established pattern.

3. *Timely.* A monthly report must be issued as soon after the close of the month as is humanly possible. With fresh information, a manager can take prompt action to correct a problem or exploit an opportunity revealed by the report.

The work of preparing these monthly reports is complicated by the fact that one expense item will be used either in part or in total in more than one budget-comparison report. Consider the case of the packaged foods company that purchases flour in bulk because it uses a great deal of flour as a raw material. Flour will appear as an expense item in the production supervisors' cost-center reports, in the brand managers' profit-center reports, and in both division and corporate management ROI reports. Accountants thus need a way to keep their numbers straight to ensure completeness and accuracy and speed preparation of all these reports. The way they do it is called "account coding." (The statement of all account codes used in an organization is called its chart of accounts.)

Accounts "tag" or label the dollar amount of each item of revenue or expense with a code number. Although this code number may have as many as 13 digits, it usually consists of at least four groups of digits. Each group of digits identifies a different organizational entity or revenue or expense item. Let's look at a sample account-code number from a fairly large corporation consisting of a number of companies, many with divisions:

11—22—444—3333

The first two digits identify the *company* whose books carry the revenue or expense item being processed. The second group identifies the *operating division.* The third names the *responsibility center,* and the fourth is for the *bookkeeping account.* With an account code like this (counting 0 as a number), the corporation can have up to 100 companies, 100 divisions, 1,000 responsibility centers within each division, and 10,000 separate accounts in their bookkeeping system.

Let's take a simple example: The cough-drop brand manager decides to test the idea of enclosing pocket calendars in each package. He orders 100,000 of these at one penny each, for a total cost of $1,000. These are delivered, and the bill is forwarded to accounting. The accountant, following standard double-entry bookkeeping practice, knows that this purchase will need two entries—a credit (Cr.) to sales promotion and a debit (Dr.) to accounts payable. These journal entries will be coded as follows:

Dr. $1,000 .... 03 — 06 — 083 — 0102
Cr. $1,000 .... 03 — 06 — 083 — 7501

In this example, 03 is the marketing and selling company; 06 is the confectionery division. The third group, 083, is the cough-drop profit center. The fourth groups of digits are different: 0102 is accounts payable—miscellaneous, and 7501 is sales promotion—consumer.

The way a company codes its accounts is up to its controller and will depend both on company size and on the number and types of reports that have to be prepared. Account coding is rarely the same from one company to another; thus, when two companies merge or when one company acquires another, one of the first accounting jobs involved is to change the account coding of one company to match the other's. For simplicity, the smaller company usually changes its code.

The manager who wants to know how his expense and income items are coded, and the way in which his company's account code is organized, should get in touch with someone in the controller's department. ■

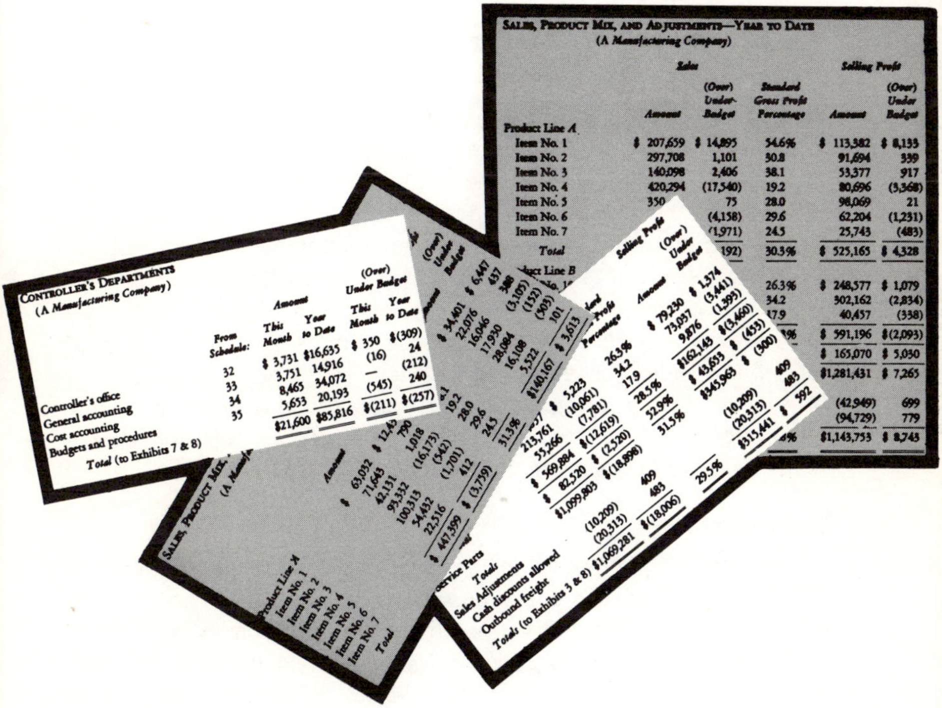

SALES, PRODUCT MIX, AND ADJUSTMENTS—YEAR TO DATE
(A Manufacturing Company)
CONTROLLER'S DEPARTMENTS
(A Manufacturing Company)

Chapter 4.
Types of costs and their behavior

So far, we've looked at the benefits, purposes, and varieties of budgeting systems, as well as the elements of responsibility accounting systems set up for budgeting purposes. Since budgets invariably concern themselves with costs, let's explore various cost concepts—including types of costs and their behavior.

Types of costs

Costs are characterized in terms of their response to levels of activity, as the following definitions show.

Variable Costs. Costs that vary with each unit of activity are called, not surprisingly, *variable costs.* Raw material is perhaps the best illustration of a variable cost; with each unit manufactured, raw material cost varies directly. If 20 percent more units are manufactured, then raw material costs (assuming there has been no increase in the cost of the raw material) will increase by 20 percent.

Semivariable Costs. Some costs vary with the amount of an activity, but not in a direct relationship to it. Such costs are called semivariable costs; they are "almost" variable. Semivariable costs differ from variable costs in that they do not vary directly with each unit of activity.

Maintenance costs are a common example of semivariable costs. For most machinery, there is a minimum maintenance cost that is independent of how much the machinery is used and, in addition, a maintenance expense that varies with machine usage. For example, most machines with moving parts that operate 96 hours per week will need more maintenance than those that operate 16 hours, but probably only four times as much rather than six. The cost varies with the activity, but not in a direct relationship.

Fixed Costs. As the name suggests, "fixed costs" remain the same regardless of the level of activity. A plant's property taxes and the depreciation expense on its equipment are typical examples of fixed costs. The expense remains the same regardless of the level of activity or the number of units produced.

We should note that fixed costs, like almost any other in today's world of double-digit inflation, can increase. They are therefore not fixed in the sense that they may never increase or decrease. Rather, they do not increase or decrease in relation to the level of activity, as do the variable and semivariable costs described above.

The Total Cost Matrix. The total cost of any activities or organizations is always made up of either variable, semivariable, or fixed costs—and, usually, a combination of all three.

Types of costs and the budgeting process

While any text on basic economic theory will deal with the concepts of variable, semivariable, and fixed costs, these ideas have more than a theoretical application to the budgeting process.

We've said that a budget is a plan, or target. To develop a budget, it is necessary to determine or forecast (1) the expected level of activity (that is, what units will be manufactured and/or sold) and (2) An estimate of how costs will respond to these activities—and at what amounts. In short, the budget must reflect the planned activity and the fixed, semivariable, and variable costs resulting from that activity.

To illustrate the point, let's return to Joe, supervisor of the cough-drop line mentioned earlier. After receiving a sizable inheritance from his aunt's estate, Joe decided to give up his job and go into business for himself—manufacturing and selling widgets. Here is some information concerning the conduct of his business:

1. Joe will manufacture the widgets in a small building, which he will rent for $300 per month or $3,600 per year. All utilities are included.

2. Joe purchased a widget-molding machine for $12,000, installed. The estimated useful life is ten years. On a straight-line basis (equal amounts each of the ten years), the annual depreciation charge is $1,200.

3. The cost of materials for each widget is $10.

4. Joe needs one attendant to run the widget-making machine. His weekly wages and benefits amount to $200.

5. Joe has obtained a distributor who will charge a sales commission of 10 percent for each widget sold.

6. The distributor estimates that during the year he can sell 6,000 widgets at a price of $20 each.

7. Joe plans to pay himself a salary of $1,000 per month to manage his new company.

8. Packaging material for each widget costs $1.00.

9. At full capacity, 4 widgets per hour can be manufactured. During a 40-hour week, a total of 160 widgets can be produced.

10. The widget machine Joe has purchased must be cleaned and overhauled after every 100 hours of operation or every month, whichever occurs first. The manufacturer provides this service at a flat cost of $200 per overhaul.

Joe has accumulated the facts and plans about his business and is now in a position to develop a budget for his widget business for the forthcoming year. As we've indicated, the first step is a determination of the types and amounts of activities that will take place. For Joe's simple widget business this is not difficult—and we can see that Joe plans to manufacture and sell 6,000 widgets.

Joe's next step is to determine how the costs of his business will behave in relation to the sales and manufacturing activities he plans. See Exhibit 7, page **43**, for the way in which Joe (or, for that matter, any supervisor) might determine such cost behavior. After figuring out these cost relationships, Joe can take the specific estimates of activity and expense and translate them into an operating budget, as shown in Exhibit 8, page **44**.

Despite the simplicity of Joe's hypothetical widget business, the *basic* approach to the development of a budget is the same no matter how much more complex the operation. And the possible benefits of that process are the same for Joe's widget business as for any other organization. For example, after translating a few basic facts about his simple business into a "budget," Joe can use it to:

1. *Anticipate and define possible problems.* Joe may conclude that the projected profitability of his widget business is unsatisfactory and that to improve it he will need more sales, fewer expenses, or both.

Exhibit 7: Cost categories as determined by sales and manufacturing activities

Cost Description	Fixed	Semi-Vari-able	Varies with	Vari-able	Varies with
Building Rent	X				
Depreciation	X				
Raw Material				X	Units Manufactured
Wages for Labor	X*				
Joe's Salary	X				
Packaging Material				X	Units Packaged
Maintenance		X	Units Manufactured		
Sales Commissions				X	Units Sold

* Wages would be variable if they were paid on a piece-rate basis—as is the case in some companies.

2. *Measure the adequacy of actual performance.* If Joe finds the business prospects reflected in his budget to be satisfactory, he can use that budget (broken down into interim periods) as a basis for comparison against the actual results as they take place during the year. In this way, he can determine whether his sales, expense, and income goals are being realized—and, if not, what corrective steps he needs to take.

Other cost concepts

Now let's briefly explore some additional cost concepts and definitions useful for the supervisor concerned with budgets.

Direct Costs. The term *direct cost* is often used synonymously with the term *variable cost* as it has been defined earlier in this section. The cost of material varies *directly* with each unit manufactured; a variable cost, it is also a direct cost because it can be directly and specifically identified with the particular unit manufactured. In this instance, and any other, a variable cost would be a direct cost. The variability of the cost, however, is not the factor that distinguishes it as a direct cost. Rather, the critical distinction lies in the cost's *direct* association with the particular unit involved.

Exhibit 8: Joe's operating budget

Budgeted Revenue (estimated):		Per Year
Annual Sales of 6,000 widgets at $20 per unit		*$120,000*
Budgeted Expenses:		
Variable Expenses		
Raw Material—$10 per unit times 6,000 units to be manufactured.	60,000	
Packaging Material—$1 per unit times 6,000 units to be manufactured and packaged.	6,000	
Sales Commissions— 10% commission per unit at $20 equals $2 per unit times 6,000 units.	12,000	
Subtotal—Variable Costs	*78,000*	
Semivariable Expenses		
Maintenance Expense— 6,000 units to be manufactured at capacity of 4 units per hour will require 1,500 hours of machine operation. Maintenance is required every 100 hours of operation, so 15 overhauls will be required at $200 per overhaul for a total annual cost of $3,000.		
Subtotal—Semivariable Costs	*3,000*	
Fixed Costs		
Rent	3,600	
Depreciation	1,200	
Labor—Annual Wages for Widget Machine Attendant	10,400	
Administration—Joe's Salary	12,000	
Subtotal—Fixed Costs	*27,200*	
Total All Costs		*$108,200*
Income Before Taxes (Sales Minus Total Costs)		*$ 11,800*

Direct costs in this context can also be semivariable or fixed. They are referred to as direct costs because they can be directly identified with any given activity or responsibility center.

Advertising, for example, is not a variable cost—but it would be considered a direct cost and presented as such in assessing the profitability of a product line. The same would be true for the costs of brand management and market research associated with the support of that product.

More often than not, maintenance is a semivariable expense—but if that maintenance cost is incurred exclusively on machines that manufacture a product, it would be considered a direct cost for that particular product. The concept of "direct costs" can also be explained by contrasting them with "indirect costs."

Indirect Costs. As the term implies, indirect costs *cannot* be identified with any particular activity or product. Typical examples of indirect costs are the expenses associated with the corporate president's office, the corporate secretary's office, and the corporate controller's department. Although the costs of these functions and activities are critical to the overall conduct of company business, it is usually difficult to *directly* associate any one of them with a particular product or particular segment of the company. They are nonetheless necessary costs that must be taken into account in selling products and assessing profitability. Since they can't be directly associated with any specific activity, they are often "allocated." Quite literally, *to allocate* means *to place* or *apportion*—and usually this is just what happens. Indirect costs are apportioned to products, branches, factories, divisions, or other company elements on one basis or another. The bases or combination of bases for these allocations are numerous and, while there is no "correct" base, here are some of the more common ones:

- The sales total of a product or division in relation to total company sales.
- The direct costs of a product or division in relation to the total direct costs of all company products and/or divisions.
- The assets related to a product or division in relation to total company assets.
- The number of employees in a division in relation to the total number of employees in the company.

All the above methods rely upon a set formula for allocation. Often, however, indirect costs are based upon "time or effort" allocations. Under this system, the group generating the indirect costs estimates (or sometimes actually records) the time and effort they devote to their particular segment of the company. Thus, the corporate legal counsel may indicate that he devotes 60 percent of his time to the "consumer products division," 25 percent to the "industrial products division," and 15 percent to the "specialty products division." Each division is charged accordingly.

Later on, we'll analyze more thoroughly the relevance of indirect costs in various business decisions. Our purpose at the moment is to acquaint you with these concepts, for they have come to play an increasing role in the design of various budget systems. A typical example of their application might appear in such a format as shown in Exhibit 9, page **47**.

So far, we have dealt with cost concepts and types of cost behavior in very general terms. Let's now look at the treatment of those same ideas, as well as some others, in formal accounting and budgeting systems.

Types of costs in manufacturing cost accounting

At the outset of a discussion of cost accounting (or manufacturing cost accounting) it is useful to differentiate between the cost accounting process of the merchandiser and that of the manufacturer.

When a merchant purchases a product and then resells it, the accounting—like the transaction—is rather simple and straightforward. To determine the cost of the goods sold, he needs only to keep a record of the prices at which he sells and purchases the merchandise. The manufacturer differs from the merchant—he *makes* the product he sells. As with Joe's widgets, the manufacturer takes some raw material and then fabricates or converts it. This process gives rise to three common types of manufacturing costs.

Material Costs. Material costs are the costs of the materials used to make the product. Again, material costs are variable costs.

Labor Costs. These, obviously, are the costs of labor used to manufacture the product.

Factory Overhead. These are often fixed costs associated with the manufacture of the product. In Joe's widget business, the depreciation of the widget-making machine would clearly be factory overhead, as would the major portion of the monthly rental of the building in which the widgets are manufactured.

In addition to the costs of material, labor, and factory overhead, the manufacturer also incurs costs in selling his product and administering the overall business. These costs are commonly called selling expenses and general and administrative expenses. The five basic types of costs are shown in Exhibit 10, page **48**.

Exhibit 9: Sample application of direct and indirect costs

	Consumer Division	Industrial Division	Specialty Division
Sales	*$500,000*	*$350,000*	*$100,000*
Less			
Direct Variable and Semi-variable Manufacturing Costs	310,000	200,000	40,000
Subtotal	*190,000*	*150,000*	*60,000*
Less			
Direct Fixed Manufacturing Costs	40,000	50,000	20,000
Gross Margin	*150,000*	*100,000*	*40,000*
Less			
Direct Selling Expenses	50,000	18,000	12,000
Direct Administrative Expenses	25,000	10,000	5,000
Total Direct S&A Expenses	*75,000*	*28,000*	*17,000*
Subtotal—Division Contribution	*75,000*	*72,000*	*23,000*
Less			
Indirect Selling Expenses	20,000	25,000	2,000
Indirect Administrative Expenses	5,000	10,000	1,000
Total Indirect S&A Expenses	*25,000*	*35,000*	*3,000*
Subtotal—Division Income Before Tax and Interest	*$ 50,000*	*$ 37,000*	*$ 20,000*

A major problem for the cost accountant is that fixed expenses categorized under factory overhead are often similar to those under general and administrative expenses—and even, sometimes, similar to those under selling expenses as well. To put the problem another way, it is often hard to choose a category for a particular expense.

Take Joe's widget business, for example. Is the salary that Joe

Exhibit 10: Basic cost elements

	Cost of Merchandiser	Cost of Manufacturer
Direct Labor		X
Direct Material		X
Factory Overhead		X
General and Administrative Expenses	X	X
Selling Expenses	X	X

pays himself part of factory overhead—or, since he is general manager, is it an administrative expense? Perhaps some of it is a selling expense, since Joe is also concerned with this activity. In reality, Joe's salary probably involves all three types of expense. As a practical matter, Joe's salary could be divided (allocated) in some manner; and even if it weren't, Joe's business is so small that the issue isn't material. However, it does illustrate the difficulty of arriving at a *precise* delineation between factory overhead and general and administrative expense.

Let's explore some additional ramifications of this problem.

Product vs. Period Expenses. Exhibit 11, page **49**, shows the same five general kinds of expenses shown in Exhibit 10, but they have been separated into two groups: product expenses and period expenses. Product expenses are those that vary with each unit of activity or each product made (many product expenses are therefore variable expenses). Raw material is perhaps the best example of a product expense that is also a variable expense.

Labor expense, on the other hand, is often a fixed or semivariable cost (although it would be a variable cost if labor were paid on a piece-rate basis—that is, so much pay for each unit assembled or manufactured). Still, labor expense is almost always considered a product expense so long as it can be directly identified with the manufacture of the product.

Period costs are almost always fixed or semivariable costs that recur during any given time period regardless of activity level. Joe, for example, must pay the same rent on his factory building whether he makes and sells one widget or 100 widgets. Period costs are in

Exhibit 11: Cost elements and their accounting treatment

Cost Elements	Cost of Merchandiser	Cost of Manufacturer	Clear-Cut Product Costs	Clear-Cut Period Costs	Period and Product Cost	Accounting Treatment
Direct Labor		×	×			Product
Direct Material		×	×			Product
Factory Overhead		×			×	Product
						some division made as to product vs. period
General and Administrative Expenses	×	×			×	Period
Selling Expenses	×	×		×		Period

Exhibit 12: Costs involved in production and sales

EZ CORPORATION

Production for Period: 10 Units (Machine Tools)
Sales for Period: 6 Units (Machine Tools)

Costs to Produce 10 and Sell 6 Units

Labor	$ 500,000
Material	400,000
Overhead	
Factory / General and Administrative	1,000,000
Selling	200,000

the nature of the indirect costs discussed earlier. The accountant can only assign these indirect costs to a period of time—usually on the basis of when they were incurred.

As Exhibit 11 and previous comments suggest, the similarity between the kinds of expenses categorized as factory overhead and those categorized as general and administrative expenses makes it difficult to differentiate precisely between what is a period cost and what is a product cost. In reality, these expenses are probably a bit of both. In manufacturing accounting, however, the accountant must make a choice—and the manner in which he does so can have a significant influence on the net income reported. We'll explore this idea more specifically—but first, a few basic facts regarding the accounting process for inventories and cost of goods sold.

Accounting for inventories and cost of goods sold

As an asset is consumed in a business, it becomes an expense. When a merchandiser purchases goods, they become an asset called "inventory." At the time that they are sold and turned over to the customer, they become an expense called "cost of goods sold."

The manufacturer also has finished goods inventories, but unlike the merchandiser, he makes them instead of purchasing them. The dollar values that he assigns to his inventory and to his cost of goods sold reflect his assessment of what it costs him to make these products. (We have already noted that the basic cost elements are those of material, labor, and factory overhead.)

But we know that the differentiation between factory overhead and general and administrative expense is, at best, imprecise. If

Exhibit 13: Calculation of cost of goods sold, factory overhead, and general and administrative expenses

EZ CORPORATION

Cost of Goods Sold (10 Units)

	Case A		Case B	
	Total	Per Unit	Total	Per Unit
Labor	$ 500,000	$ 50,000	$ 500,000	$ 50,000
Materials	400,000	40,000	400,000	40,000
Overhead				
80% × $1,000,000	800,000	80,000		
50% × $1,000,000			500,000	50,000
Totals	$1,700,000	$170,000	$1,400,000	$140,000

Factory Overhead and General and Administrative Expenses

	Case A	Case B
Overhead: Factory, General and Administrative	$1,000,000	$1,000,000
Designated as Factory Overhead	800,000	500,000
Balance, Designated as General and Administrative Expenses for the Period	$ 200,000	$ 500,000

the accountant decides that some of the expenses in the area of imprecision are product costs, then these costs will be reflected as part of the manufacturer's inventory. Thus, until the products are sold, product costs are shown as inventory, an asset, rather than as an expense. But if he decides that the expense in question is a *period* cost, it is shown as an expense rather than an asset for the accounting period. To illustrate this, let's look at EZ Corporation and see the different financial results the company can obtain from the same manufacturing costs as a result of different decisions that might be made regarding period *vs.* product costs.

As indicated in Exhibit 12, the distinction between factory over-

Exhibit 14: Calculation of net income based on sale of 6 units

EZ CORPORATION

	Case A		Case B	
	Per Unit	Total	Per Unit	Total
Sales Revenue (6 units)	*$250,000*	*$1,500,000*	*$250,000*	*$1,500,000*
Less Cost of Goods Sold (6 units)	170,000	1,020,000	140,000	840,000
Gross Margin	*$ 80,000*	*$ 480,000*	*$110,000*	*$ 660,000*
Less				
Selling Expenses		200,000		200,000
General and Administrative Expenses		200,000		500,000
Subtotal		*400,000*		*700,000*
Net Income/Loss Before Taxes		*$ 80,000*		*($ 40,000)*
Value of Inventory Shown on Balance Sheet at End of Accounting Period (4 units)		$ 680,000		$ 560,000

head and general and administrative expenses is unclear. In Exhibit 13, p. 51, the accountant assumes in Case A that 80 percent of the overhead costs are product costs. In Case B he assumes that only 50 percent of them are product costs. Exhibit 14, above, shows how these two assumptions affect the calculation of the cost of goods sold and the asset inventories for the period in each case. It also shows, for each, net income for the period on the basis of sales volume.

We'll leave unanswered the problem of whether the company makes money. In practice, accountants would obviously have to arrive at a consensus. And in fact they do, every time a financial statement is issued. Knowing what's involved, we can understand that arriving at such results is as much an art as a science. ■

Chapter 5.

Manufacturing cost systems and the contribution concept

Some knowledge of how various costs are treated under different accounting systems is necessary for the meaningful, intelligent use of cost information in the budgeting process. Although the cost concepts and behavior we discussed are basic, they provide sufficient background for a brief, general discussion of three different types of manufacturing cost systems: absorption cost systems, direct cost systems, and standard cost systems.

Absorption cost systems

Full costing is another name for absorption costing. Under absorption cost systems, all three elements of manufacturing costs that we have discussed—direct labor, direct material, and factory overhead—are charged to (or absorbed by) the product. Under this approach, all three basic costs figure as "product" expenses. None of them is taken as a period cost.

Absorption costing is the most conventional approach to manufacturing cost accounting. Under full absorption cost accounting, inventories on the balance sheet always include an element of factory overhead. This factory overhead will not be reflected as an expense in the income statement until the product is sold. We've already commented on some of the complications and implications of defining factory overhead costs that must be assigned to products under an absorption costing system.

Direct costing systems

Absorption cost accounting systems are required for governmental and public financial reporting. However, the continuing emphasis on the use of accounting data for managerial control purposes has led in recent years to an alternative method of manufacturing cost accounting called "direct cost accounting." Since direct cost accounting is almost always used exclusively for internal control purposes, it serves as a supplementary accounting system.

The principle of direct cost accounting is simple. Only expenses that can be clearly and directly identified with the manufacture of each product are charged as a cost of that product. Such expenses are usually limited to direct material and labor costs. Thus, under the direct cost system, the complexities and vagaries involved in allocating overhead between products and periods are eliminated.

Exhibit 15, page 56, illustrates the accounting treatment of direct versus absorption costing systems. Exhibit 16 (page 57) shows that under direct costing, the elements of manufacturing and overhead are charged to the period in which they were incurred rather than to the product. Under this approach, net income for the period varies more directly with sales activity. Advocates of the direct costing system argue that this is in fact one of its benefits, since it is more logical for a firm's net income to respond to sales activity rather than to production activity. It is further argued that the whole process of overhead allocation to products is difficult and clouds rather than clari-

Exhibit 15: Accounting treatment of direct versus absorption costs

EZ CORPORATION

	Accounting Period 1		*Accounting Period 2*
Production in Units	10		10
Sales in Units	6		14
Sales Price per Unit	$250,000		$250,000
Costs			
Labor		$500,000	
Material		400,000	
Factory Overhead*		500,000	
General and Administrative Expenses		500,000	
Selling Expenses		200,000	

* Factory overhead and general and administrative expenses have been distributed as per Case B in Exhibit 13.

Factory Overhead Unit Cost

Period	*Total Factory Overhead Cost*	*Units Produced*	*Factory Overhead Per Unit*
1	$500,000	10	$50,000
2	500,000	10	50,000

Unit Cost	*Absorption*	*Direct*
Labor	$ 50,000	$50,000
Material	40,000	40,000
Factory Overhead	50,000	0
Totals	$140,000	$90,000

Costs of Goods Sold

		Absorption Costing		*Direct Costing*	
Period	*Sales Units*	*Per Unit*	*For Period*	*Per Unit*	*For Period*
1	6	$140,000	$ 840,000	$90,000	$ 540,000
2	14	140,000	1,960,000	90,000	1,260,000
Totals	20		$2,800,000		$1,800,000

fies financial results. (Later on, we will explore this notion further in discussing the "contribution concept.")

Standard costing

The concept of standard costing also permits a more effective use of accounting data for managerial purposes. Up to this point, manufacturing costs have been discussed only in terms of those actually recorded in the official accounting records of the manufacturing enterprise. Of necessity, this information was historical—that is, it told management only what costs were. In contrast, the idea behind stan-

Exhibit 16: Comparison of net income calculated under direct versus absorption accounting

EZ CORPORATION

	Absorption Costing		*Direct Costing*	
	Period 1	*Period 2*	*Period 1*	*Period 2*
Sales Units	6	14	6	14
Revenue	*$1,500,000*	*$3,500,000*	*$1,500,000*	*$3,500,000*
Less				
Labor	300,000	700,000	300,000	700,000
Material	240,000	560,000	240,000	560,000
Factory Overhead	300,000	700,000	0	0
Cost of Goods Sold	*840,000*	*1,960,000*	*540,000*	*1,260,000*
Gross Margin	*$ 660,000*	*$1,540,000*	*$ 960,000*	*$2,240,000*
Less				
Factory Overhead	0	0	500,000	500,000
Selling Expenses	200,000	200,000	200,000	200,000
General and Administrative Expenses	500,000	500,000	500,000	500,000
Total Expenses	*$ 700,000*	*$ 700,000*	*$1,200,000*	*$1,200,000*
Net Income/(Loss)	*($ 40,000)*	*$ 840,000*	*($ 240,000)*	*$1,040,000*
Cumulative Net Income	$800,000		$800,000	
Ending Inventory				
Units	4	0	4	0
Value	$ 560,000	0	$ 360,000	0

dard costing is to provide management with information on what costs *should* be, rather than simply what they were.

As a benchmark for measuring efficiency, they must be well-thought-out and accurate. For this reason, they are actually often determined through time-and-motion studies of exactly how much money should be spent on raw materials and how much labor should be expended on making each product—always, of course, under well-managed conditions. Sometimes, standard costs are built up on the basis of past experience.

Once the standard has been developed—under whatever approach—all that is required is to record the total number of physical units manufactured during a given period and then apply the standard cost rate to this volume of production. Many supervisors undoubtedly encounter standard costs as an integral part of their work. Standard costs are often used in budgeting; indeed, in a sense the standard cost is tantamount to a budget—it is after all a target, or criterion of efficiency.

Remember that even when standard costs are used, they do not replace so-called actual costs. Instead, actual costs are recorded and then compared with the standard—and the difference is shown as a favorable or unfavorable variance. If actual costs are greater than the standard ones developed, the variance is unfavorable. Conversely, if the actual costs are less than standard, the variance is favorable. Exhibit 17, page 59, shows how the net income for a company might be recorded under a standard costing system.

The particular appeal of standard costs is that they provide a warning system that allows management to spot and take action more quickly than might be possible under an actual cost system. (Note again the similarity between a standard costing system and a budget; both provide a benchmark for performance.)

Another advantage is that standard costs can simplify the accounting process for companies that manufacture a high volume of items with a complex product mix incorporating similar ingredients or machines. In such cases, it is extremely difficult if not impractical to record the costs incurred—so standards are used because they can simply be taken and applied against the total volume produced. The actual costs can then be taken on a gross total basis and compared with the standard. Always, we must note, final net income is based on the *actual* cost, not the standard cost. A standard cost system can involve standards only for direct costs and/or absorption costs.

Two current economic phenomena—spiraling inflation and sky-

Exhibit 17: Typical income statement under standard costs

Sales	*$5,000,000*
Less	
Cost of Goods Sold at Standard Rate	2,800,000
Variances*	400,000
Cost of Goods Sold	*3,200,000*
Gross Profit	*1,800,000*
Less	
Selling Expenses	400,000
General and Administrative Expenses	1,000,000
Total Expenses	*1,400,000*
Net Income Before Taxes	*$ 400,000*
*Variances	
Material Variance (higher cost)	$ 200,000
Labor Variance (higher cost)	$ 200,000

rocketing commodity prices—have complicated if not prohibited the effective use of standard costing systems, at least under current conditions. The establishment and use of a standard presumes some reasonable ability to anticipate and forecast events. In normal times, for example, when engineers established a material cost standard, they could determine rather precisely the amount of material required under efficient manufacturing conditions. They could also, under normal conditions, obtain some estimate of the expected cost at various future times. From these two factors they would then derive the material cost standard. But if the material prices involved were to increase unexpectedly at rates in excess of 300 percent—as, in fact, some did in 1974—the standard would lose much of its usefulness as a norm for efficiency.

The preceding discussion of the treatment of costs under different accounting systems will help in using cost information in the budgeting process. It also sets the stage for an examination of the "contribution concept."

The contribution concept

The contribution concept is at the heart of business decisions based on budget and cost considerations involved in various alternatives. In essence, the contribution method simply sorts out costs in terms of their behavior (fixed, semivariable, or variable) and their nature (direct or indirect) in order to arrive at intelligent business decisions concerning such questions as the following:

1. Should a certain sales territory be closed?
2. Should another sales territory be expanded?
3. Should a certain product be dropped?
4. Should a certain special sales order be taken?

Let's return to Joe's widget business to take a closer look at some of these ideas. For the sake of convenience, we are reprinting in Exhibit 18, page 61, Joe's operating budget. As you can see in Exhibit 18, Joe is selling his widgets at $20 each. Let's suppose that he has an offer to sell an additional thousand, but at a price of $15 each. The obvious question: Should he?

From his budget, we know that Joe expects to incur annual expenses of $108,200 to manufacture and sell 6,000 widgets. For the sake of simplicity, we assume that all these costs are associated with the manufacture of widgets (that is, they are all product costs). Therefore, the cost per widget under the absorption cost concept would be:

$$\frac{\text{Costs}}{\text{Widgets}} \quad \frac{\$108{,}200}{6{,}000} = \$18.03 \text{ per widget}$$

If each widget costs $18.03 to manufacture, but can be sold under special order at only $15, it would certainly seem that Joe should decline the order. This rather superficial but nonetheless conventional analysis ignores the various types of cost behavior and will probably lead Joe to the wrong decision. While it's true that Joe's total costs are $108,200 to make 6,000 widgets, we know that $27,200 of these are fixed and $3,000 are semivariable. The calculation of a total cost of $18.03 per unit and its use to make this particular decision assumes that all costs are variable—which is, of course, not true for Joe's business or any other.

Under the contribution concept, Joe's proposal would be analyzed in terms of exactly what costs would vary with (or be directly associated with) the decision to manufacture and sell 1,000 widgets at a price of $15 per widget. Exhibit 19, page 62, specifically illustrates the contribution approach to the analysis of this proposal.

When the proposal is analyzed in the above manner, we can see that instead of losing money on it, Joe would actually have a contribution to fixed expenses and a net income of $2 per unit. Based on the order of 1,000 widgets, Joe's profits will actually be $2,000 greater than if he doesn't accept the order. The reason, of course,

Exhibit 18: Joe's operating budget

Budgeted Revenue (estimated):		Per Year
Annual Sales of 6,000 widgets at $20 per unit		*$120,000*
Budgeted Expenses:		
Variable Expenses		
Raw Material—$10 per unit times 6,000 units to be manufactured.	60,000	
Packaging Material—$1 per unit times 6,000 units to be manufactured and packaged.	6,000	
Sales Commissions— 10% commission per unit at $20 equals $2 per unit times 6,000 units.	12,000	
Subtotal—Variable Costs	*78,000*	
Semivariable Expenses		
Maintenance Expense— 6,000 units to be manufactured at capacity of 4 units per hour will require 1,500 hours of machine operation. Maintenance is required every 100 hours of operation, so 15 overhauls will be required at $200 per overhaul for a total annual cost of $3,000.		
Subtotal—Semivariable Costs	*3,000*	
Fixed Costs		
Rent	3,600	
Depreciation	1,200	
Labor—Annual Wages for Widget Machine Attendant	10,400	
Administration—Joe's Salary	12,000	
Subtotal—Fixed Costs	*27,200*	
Total All Costs		*$108,200*
Income Before Taxes (Sales Minus Total Costs)		*$ 11,800*

Exhibit 19: Contribution analysis of the per-unit profitability of Joe's special widget order

Revenue per Unit		*$15.00*
Less: Variable and Semivariable Unit Costs		
Raw Material	$10.00	
Packaging Material	1.00	
Sales Commission—10% on $15 per Widget	1.50	
Maintenance Expense	.50	
Total Variable and Semivariable Costs		*13.00*
Unit Contribution to Fixed Expenses and Profit		*$ 2.00*

Note: Above figures are taken from Joe's operating budget, shown in Exhibit 18. Maintenance expense is calculated as follows: Cost per overhaul ($200) divided by hours of operation requiring overhaul (100) equals an average maintenance expense of $2 per hour. Since 4 units are produced per hour, $2 divided by 4 equals a per-unit maintenance cost of 50¢.

is that his fixed costs will not increase as a result of the new business. Thus, the contribution will actually be a straight contribution or increase in net income, and it would appear that Joe should take the order.

For Joe or any other businessman in a similar situation, there is an additional critical consideration. This is supposedly a special order for Joe—but before he fills it, he needs to consider whether his other customers might request widgets at a price of $15 rather than $20. Should this be the case, Joe's one decision that made sense over the short term could spell disaster for his business over the long term.

Variable or direct costs are also often referred to as marginal costs, and contribution as marginal income. Direct costing and contribution analysis have been one of the most significant developments in management accounting techniques. But this tool, like any other, cannot be used blindly. There's an old saying that many businesses have gone to their grave "dancing to the magic music of marginal costs."

Other applications of the contribution concept

The simplicity of Joe's widget business facilitates an explanation of the contribution concept, but the basic idea remains the same however complex the problem or organization. Let's look at some applications in situations more likely to be encountered by the successful manager in a larger business organization, EZ Corporation.

Assume, for example, that management wants to review the profitability of various sales territories (a likely action in a time such as the present) and are presented with the conventional information for this purpose (shown in Exhibit 20, below). Looking at this information, management is likely to conclude that region C was unprofitable and region B marginal.

Under the contribution concept, the same information would be presented as in Exhibit 21, p. 64. The similarity to Joe's special widget order is obvious—an analysis based on the contribution concept changes our perception of the comparative profitability of the

Exhibit 20: Analysis of sales region profitability

EZ CORPORATION

	Region A	Region B	Region C	Total
Sales	*$500,000*	*$300,000*	*$200,000*	*$1,000,000*
Less				
Cost of Goods Sold[1]	300,000	200,000	150,000	650,000
Gross Margin	*200,000*	*100,000*	*50,000*	*350,000*
Less				
Transportation Expenses	25,000	30,000	15,000	70,000
Sales Commissions	40,000	25,000	10,000	75,000
Selling Expenses[2]	60,000	20,000	30,000	110,000
Administrative Expenses[2]	30,000	20,000	10,000	60,000
Expense Subtotal	*155,000*	*95,000*	*65,000*	*315,000*
Operating Profit/(Loss)	*$ 45,000*	*$ 5,000*	*($ 15,000)*	*$ 35,000*

[1] All goods produced at central manufacturing location. Figures include head office allocations of indirect manufacturing fixed overhead.

[2] Include head office allocations of indirect fixed expenses as follows:

	Region A	Region B	Region C	Total
Selling	$15,000	$15,000	$15,000	$45,000
Administrative	5,000	5,000	5,000	15,000
Total	*$20,000*	*$20,000*	*$20,000*	*$60,000*

sales regions. Even though the problem is different, the basic approach is the same—namely, to identify specific cost behavior and determine the directness of its association with the activity (or decision) being analyzed. In the case of EZ Corporation, we can note that all the regions have a rather sizable contribution to indirect fixed expenses. But how about region C, which showed a loss in the analysis in Exhibit 20? If management decided on that basis to close it, contribution analysis shows that—even with the region's direct fixed

Exhibit 21: Contribution analysis by sales region

EZ CORPORATION

	Region A	Region B	Region C	Total
Sales	*$500,000*	*$300,000*	*$200,000*	*$1,000,000*
Less				
Variable Costs				
Production	250,000	160,000	75,000	485,000
Marketing				
Transportation	25,000	30,000	15,000	70,000
Commissions	40,000	25,000	10,000	75,000
Total Variable Costs	*315,000*	*215,000*	*100,000*	*630,000*
Contribution After Variable Costs	*185,000*	*85,000*	*100,000*	*370,000*
Less				
Direct Fixed Costs[1]				
Selling	45,000	5,000	15,000	65,000
Administrative	25,000	15,000	5,000	45,000
Total Direct Fixed Costs	*70,000*	*20,000*	*20,000*	*110,000*
Region Contribution	*$115,000*	*$ 65,000*	*$ 80,000*	*$ 260,000*
Less				
Indirect Fixed Expenses				
Manufacturing				165,000
Selling				45,000
Administrative				15,000
Total Indirect Fixed Expenses				*225,000*
Operating Profit				*$ 35,000*

[1] Direct fixed costs by region were obtained by deducting allocations of fixed selling and administrative expenses in Note 2, Exhibit 20.

Exhibit 22: Analysis of contribution by product

EZ CORPORATION

	Product X	Product Y	Product Z	Total
Sales	*$230,000*	*$125,000*	*$42,000*	*$397,000*
Less				
Variable Costs				
Production	125,000	70,000	20,000	215,000
Marketing—Commissions	15,000	6,000	2,000	23,000
Marketing—Transportation	7,000	2,400	500	9,900
Total Variable Costs	*147,000*	*78,400*	*22,500*	*247,900*
Contribution After Variable Costs	*83,000*	*46,600*	*19,500*	*149,100*
Less				
Direct Fixed Costs				
Production	0	0	0	0
Marketing	10,000	8,000	3,000	21,000
Total Direct Fixed Costs	*10,000*	*8,000*	*3,000*	*21,000*
Product Contribution	*$ 73,000*	*$ 38,600*	*$16,500*	*$128,100*
Less				
Indirect Fixed Expenses				
Manufacturing				40,000
Selling				20,000
Administrative				10,000
Total Indirect Fixed Expenses				*70,000*
Operating Profit				*$ 58,100*

costs eliminated—there would be a reduction of $80,000 in contribution to indirect corporate fixed costs (which would not, of course, be reduced) and the corporation would be thrown into a loss.

Finally, Exhibit 22 (above) shows a typical illustration of how an assessment of product profitability might be made under the contribution concept. Obviously, the essence of the contribution concept involves identifying costs by their behavior pattern. Under contribution analysis, costs relevant to the decision at hand are analyzed to determine whether—and by how much—that cost will vary as a result of the decision.

With Joe's special widget order, we saw how contribution analysis facilitated an assessment of the economic consequences of the decision he had to make. This was also true for the EZ Corporation's analysis of profitability by sales region.

For the manager, contribution analysis holds an additional attraction. From our exhibits, we can see that under the contribution concept a manager is never charged with an expense that his decision did not influence.

Compare, for example, the performance reading on sales region C in Exhibit 20 with that of the same region in Exhibit 21. In Exhibit 20, the performance of region C's manager was assessed after he had been charged with $20,000 of indirect selling and administrative expenses and $75,000 of indirect manufacturing fixed overhead. But these costs result from headquarters' decisions and actions—not his. Exhibit 21, which analyzes performance under the contribution concept, more accurately portrays his responsibility.

Controversy still surrounds the contribution (or direct cost) concept, and books continue to be written in praise or criticism of the technique. Even so, the acceptance and application of the contribution concept continues to grow. It is an essential part of any discussion or utilization of modern budgeting basics. ■

Chapter 6.
Preparing and presenting a budget plan

At this point, we have dissected all the key elements and mechanisms involved in a company's budget and performance reporting system. We have seen how the various pieces interact and how they come together into an essential management information and control system for all supervisory and management levels. We have examined various options and alternatives to show the flexibility available to management in defining the way each company activity will be measured and reported. Now let's put the whole thing together and show how a company's profit plan is constructed from start to finish. But rather than dwell on the systems that managers may have to use, let's see how managers use these tools in practice. First, we'll look at the way they go about preparing and then presenting a budget plan.

Before the beginning

Three or more months before the start of the next fiscal year, it is usual for preliminary thinking on next year's budget to begin. At lower and middle management levels, managers and supervisors begin thinking about possible ways to make their work groups more productive and efficient—in short, more profitable. This is normal and good. But in the total company situation and from the top management viewpoint, some of this activity could be misdirected if each manager assumes, as is human, that what is good or better for his responsibility center is good or better for the company. Therefore, well before budgets and plans are started for the next fiscal year, top management is responsible for reviewing and reconsidering general company goals and the general assumptions to be used as background for all planning activity.

The general goals for most well-established companies are usually obvious to all concerned and are the same for all companies. The standard philosophy that "more is better" holds. More sales, more products or fields of activity, more profit, more return—all are general goals shared by the majority of (if not all) profit-making enterprises. These goals express the philosophy of growth that springs from the belief that ceasing to grow is beginning to die.

To meet these general goals, within each company there will be general agreement on programs, general agreement on where this growth will come from. "More is better" thinking holds in this area as well. If growth has come from new product development in the past, then more research and development is accepted as a general ongoing program. If growth has come from expansion of production capacity, then the general program of increasing capacity will be tacitly in effect.

In the course of just a few months, the perceptive manager will determine for himself—from what his superiors and colleagues say or don't say and from what they do or don't do—what the general goals and agreed-upon programs are within the company. In most companies, these general goals and programs are so obvious they are never stated in a definite form. Nevertheless, each company will be better served if top management periodically states the obvious and publishes a general statement of company goals. The ideal time for this, of course, is just before the start of the planning cycle.

How much better is best?

One problem that all managers face in implementing the "more is better" philosophy is the question of how much "better" is "best." For instance, if a manager believes that workers will be happier and

more productive with a $10-a-week increase, it follows that they will be even happier with a $20-a-week raise. So why not consider a $100-a-week raise, or even more? The point is, of course, that at some point "even more" ceases to be "even better"—instead of continuing to raise productivity, further pay increases simply raise costs. At issue is the difference between the words *maximum* and *optimum.* There really is no maximum pay raise that can be given, but there is an optimum. The optimum raise is the minimum pay increase that will yield the maximum productivity increase.

Similarly, the difference between *maximum* and *optimum* is important in outlining goals. The definition of "optimum growth" and "optimum profits" will vary for each company and even for each division. Clear definition of these goals by top management can make for a more productive planning process throughout the company.

A further series of factors that come into play during the planning process are the assumptions made by each manager and supervisor. In many cases, these assumptions are made at the subconscious level and so remain unstated and unexamined. These assumptions can be quite basic. For instance:

• Raw materials will be available in the required quantity at the required time.

• Managers will be given the "tools" to do the job—that is, in order for them to deliver a specific profit, management will authorize requested needs in terms of money, people, or equipment.

The point is obvious. An unstated and unexamined assumption can be embarrassing to the manager who has built a budget around one. And hindsight is always 20/20; when something happens that contradicts an assumption, it is very clear in retrospect exactly how incorrect the assumption was.

The yearly planning cycle

At this point, the individual manager is sure of the general aims and ongoing programs or thrust of the company as a whole. He has also stated and examined for himself the assumptions he has made regarding his own area of responsibility, and he is ready to start planning in detail the specific activity of his responsibility center for the next year. But planning begins with analysis, and analysis comes from the situation and the facts.

The basics for comparison: this year

If a budget is to be approved by the beginning of the new fiscal year, it must be prepared and presented during the closing months of the preceding fiscal year. To plan for next year, and to be able to put this plan and its numerical targets into perspective, a comparison with this year's results is necessary. But this year isn't over yet; there are two, three, or more months yet to go. Obviously, the final figures for this year will have to be developed. These are usually prepared by each manager and are generally called this year's estimate.

The manager who is on top of the progress, developments, and details of his responsibility center will normally have no difficulty in pinning down the year-end totals for the various line items in his budget. He will have eight or nine months of actual results, will be in the midst of a further month, and will have to estimate results for the remaining two or three months' activity. But at this point in the year, various patterns of activity are set, production schedules and inventory or shipment forecasts are all planned. Year-end total costs can be predicted with good accuracy because actual figures for the months to date will show the trend of variances (favorable or unfavorable) to the budgeted figures.

Once the year-end estimate for his responsibility center is developed, the wise manager will compare these figures with those of his budget. There should not be any surprises in terms of performance and variances since he normally will have seen these developing earlier. But if there are surprises, it's important to have found them by himself—and, if possible, to plan their explanation and correction or exploitation. It may even be possible to do something in the remainder of the fiscal year to make the year-end estimate better in terms of variation from budget.

Let's recap briefly. The manager started the year with an approved budget. Now he has defined, in his year-end estimate, what his results will be for this year. This set of figures forms the basis for two important comparisons: how he will do this year compared with what he said he'd do, and what he wants to do next year compared with what he will do this year.

Objectives, strategies, and plans

It's time now to look at three key words: *objective, strategy,* and *plan.* A plan is the detailed outline of activities that will be undertaken to satisfy the strategy selected to reach the agreed-upon objective. A strategy is one of the several ways possible to reach an objective. An objective is a defined target or position that can be quantified; it is developed from an analysis of the situation at present and projected future developments.

An example: You find yourself in a narrow, deep, circular hole in the ground in your backyard. There is water in the hole, presently ankle high. That's the situation; however, the water level is rising about an inch a minute, which leads to the prediction that you are going to get wetter and the further prediction that if the situation continues, you risk drowning. More objectives than one are possible, but you decide on one: to get out—and fast! But how?

Several strategies come to mind. You can let the situation continue and float until you reach the top. You can climb out. You can get somebody to lower a rope or ladder down to you so that you can climb out. There are a number of strategies that would involve more people or more complicated equipment—but you select one as being most practical, efficient, and easy to implement. To implement this strategy you need a plan.

Your plan is: (1) to call out and get the attention of a person on the surface; (2) to get him to fetch the ladder hanging in the garage; (3) to have him lower the ladder into the hole; and (4) for you then to climb out.

The business situation

If business life were this clear-cut and if the options and alternatives were this few, a formalized planning system would hardly be needed. But things are rarely this obvious, even to the manager most intimately involved; and, in any event, the facts, alternatives, and recommendations need spelling out to his superiors. That's why a good management planning/budget-proposal system begins with a careful statement of the situation. Depending on the level of the responsibility center, this exposition may include sections on:

1. The international, political, and economic scene.

2. Political, regulatory, or governmental developments over the last year and an estimate or projection of short-term developments as they will affect operations of the responsibility center.

3. The general financial/economic climate and the specified financial situation of the company within which the manager will operate his center.

4. The national and regional market and market trends for the product or service.

5. The situation and trend of sales, distribution, and credit.

6. The competitive situation and activity.

7. The advertising and promotion situation for the general grouping of products or services in which the company competes, and an outline of activity in this area.

8. Internal factors within the company that have acted or will act to limit or expand, accelerate or slow down, build or remove flexibility, and so forth.

9. Other parameters and considerations.

Highlighting the changes

The key to communication of the situation is the highlighting of the changes. The basic questions that those reviewing the budget presentation will ask are: "Where have we been? Where are we today? What can be expected to happen in the market that we will have to take into account?"

One of the best ways to communicate the answers to these questions is through tables, charts, or graphs. In describing the situation of his product, for instance, it is not enough for a brand manager to state the current market share. He would be well advised to prepare a simple table or chart showing product sales and share of market for the preceding three to five years for his product, together with each key competitor and the total market. Graphic presentations showing the trend of each line of data or the difference between two numbers or totals will clarify the situation for the experienced reviewer more completely and more quickly than will pages of expository writing. In preparing an exposition of his center's situation, the supervisor or manager should develop and use this technique.

Problems and opportunities as objectives

Once the situation is defined and stated, the next step is to analyze the data to determine where problems and opportunities lie. There are almost always a number of problems whose correction will increase volume or profits. Generally, there are fewer opportunities—internal or external—whose exploitation will yield greater volume or profits. Once he lists the problems to be solved or the opportunities to be exploited, the manager has a list of objectives for his responsibility center for the coming budget period.

The obvious next step is to rank items in this list in terms of their impact on growth and profits. It will then be found that the attainment of one, two, but generally no more than three of these objectives will result in a major step forward for the budget unit in question. These, of course, are the key objectives and their attainment takes top priority. It cannot be stressed too often that the fewer the objectives selected for attack, the better. Shooting for one target is generally far more productive than shooting for two.

Another important point in the definition of an objective is that it must be specific and measurable. "To increase sales" may be a fond hope or a deep desire—but it isn't an objective. "To increase sales by 10 percent to a total of $1,000,000 by the end of the next fiscal year" is definite and specific; progress toward this target can be measured and reported over the ensuing months.

An objective can be defined fairly simply when it's a quantitative target. A qualitative objective is sometimes harder to pin down. "To make the ABC company a better place to work" is just such a fuzzy start at defining an objective. The crux of the problem is measurability. How will progress toward this target be measured? Who will determine whether the company is "a better place to work?" Executives or clerical personnel? The answer, of course, will depend on the problem or opportunity that led to the selection of this objective. To make the objective specific and measurable, it could be expressed as follows: "to convince 90 percent of the clerical employees with at least 18 months' tenure by the end of the next fiscal year that ABC company has improved its working conditions." Attainment of, and progress toward, this objective can be measured by a number of formal or informal research techniques.

The manager can get a lot of help in both the identification and the definition stage from people in other parts of the company—particularly those in research, financial analysis, and marketing analysis. The wise manager with access to people in these areas brings them in to help out early and often.

Formulating strategies and plans

Once an objective is defined, the next step is to outline the method of achieving it. The method selected is the strategy; the details of implementing this method become the plan. The plan of execution generally explains sequential steps in detail—including deadlines and even costs for each. A strategy can be stated in a few sentences; rarely can a plan be condensed to less than a page.

Many, many years ago someone said, "A problem carefully defined is half solved." This holds for the management planning process as well. The more a fairly general objective can be broken down into specific objectives for specific supportive areas, with individual strategies and plans for each, the more confidence a manager can have in attaining the overriding objective.

Consider, for example, the target of "increasing the market share by 10 points" for a packaged consumer item. The manager can be more certain of achieving this target if his planning process includes the preparation of an objective, a strategy, and a detailed plan complete with timetables in the areas of sales, distribution, trade promotion, consumer promotion, advertising (both creative and media), public relations, publicity, and so forth. If the objective were expanded to include a change in the brand's profit contribution, then additional backup objectives, strategies, and detailed plans in product design, packaging, manufacturing, warehousing, and shipping should be considered.

The planning steps

Each company will have its own timing and cycle, with one or more formal or informal meetings for each step in the process that culminates in the establishment of an approved budget for the coming year. The following brief exposition will show the basic simplicity and completeness of a typical company's budgeting procedure.

- *Step 1.* After preparing a review and analysis of the current situation, the manager involved makes a written proposal to his department head, presented in a small semiformal meeting, on the problems and opportunities he has identified as the major concerns for his area of responsibility for the coming year. This proposal and the minutes of the meeting are forwarded to division managers for their information.

• *Step 2.* This is the important "budget" meeting in which the manager presents his objectives, strategies, and proposed budget to management—in the presence of his departmental manager and the other managers in his department. Each manager has prepared and submitted in advance of the meeting a multipage document. Each orally presents the highlights and the key points of his "book." After a session of comments, questions, and discussion—much of it pointed —the manager finally emerges (in most cases) with an approved budget. The better prepared the manager was, the fewer changes are made in his budget, objectives, and strategies.

• *Step 3.* This is not a meeting at all. It is the "book" prepared for the previous step, as reviewed and amended at that meeting—with the addition of the detailed plans and timetables designed to implement the approved strategies. This book becomes the manager's "bible" for follow-through during the coming year.

Other companies, with different needs, face different situations; the steps in their planning processes will vary accordingly.

Long-range planning

In addition to their yearly budget procedure, many companies develop objectives and plans that stretch into the medium-term future —typically five years. Of necessity, these are less detailed in terms of specific plans and are more strategic (vs. tactical) in scope than a one-year budget. A five-year plan will define a company's objective in terms of its fields of activity and its position within the industry— or the fields in which it competes today or in which it wishes to compete in the future. Particularly in today's inflationary economic atmosphere, a long-range plan is an important management tool and technique. Interestingly enough, the more uncertain the economic and business climate, the more important a long-range plan becomes— despite the fact that it is all the more difficult to complete and extremely difficult to have confidence in its prediction of forthcoming situations and trends.

The line manager will not normally be involved in long-range planning. He should, however, make it a point to determine whether a long-range plan has been prepared and is in effect for his company or division. If one exists, he should of course compare his proposed objectives and targets for the coming year with those in the long-range plan. The people in higher management who will be reviewing and approving his budget plans will undoubtedly be familiar with the details of the long-range plan, so the manager must be prepared to show how his short-term plan serves the company's long-term objectives.

Getting it down on paper

Most companies have a specific format, procedure, and general timetable for the process of preparing and reviewing the budget; the manager is not likely to be surprised to receive his copy of the memo from management outlining what parts of the process must be completed by what date. This time of the business year inevitably means extra work and possibly some late nights for the manager. It is the time when he must step back and look at the "forest" instead of just worrying about the individual "trees" in his responsibility center; he must put some concentrated time and effort into forecasting developments and future results even as he continues to manage present activity. But although budget time is one of additional work, the professional manager welcomes it for the additional challenge and fulfillment it brings.

The first step is an obvious one, which is probably why it sometimes gets neglected until it pops up later to waste time and bedevil the manager. Purely mechanical and organizational, it consists of planning the work of planning and budgeting, and setting up a personal timetable for each facet of the budgeting process. This is the time when the manager asks himself a series of questions:

- Do I have all the budgeting forms I'll need and sufficient copies of each?
- Do I have a copy of last year's budget proposal and any write-ups or notes made for the budget-review meeting?
- Do I understand every number in my budget-performance reports, why they are what they are, and how accounting puts them together?
- Do I have a copy of the statement of the basic aims and objectives of my company for the coming year—and am I confident I know what they are, or should I ask for clarification to be sure my budget plans and proposal will fit the company's overall goals?
- What help or specific input will I need from people inside and outside the company—and by when?
- By when should I have which part of my total plans and budget

"package" ready for preview and discussion with my boss to be sure that I have all the pieces ready on the required dates?

• Will a series of exhibits, charts, slides, or other aids help me get my points across at the formal meeting?

Having considered these and other questions, the manager pins down the mechanical details of what he has to do by when so that he will be as ready as possible with the best plan and budget proposal possible for his area of responsibility. Then comes the personally and professionally satisfying—and enjoyable—time of planning and of condensing plans into numbers on the proposed budget.

The budget meeting

Okay . . . this is it! You are as ready as you can be for the meeting, and it is about to start. Soon you will be proposing, explaining, and defending your budget and plans for your area of responsibility. There's no time to change anything in your presentation; the numbers are typed, the exhibits prepared, the objectives and strategies all spelled out. But there is time to remind yourself of some last-minute tips:

1. *Have confidence.* Let everyone know—by what you say in the meeting, by how you say it, by the way you answer questions or ask them—that you have confidence in yourself, your professionalism, your command of your area, your plans, and your budget. In short, radiate confidence. It shouldn't be a brash or cocky kind of confidence; it should be more the quiet, unshakable kind. After all, nobody knows your responsibility center better than you do. Nobody knows the details, the problems, the opportunities of your center the way you do. You are the manager for the center; therefore, you are the expert. You don't have to be aggressive to show confidence—but do avoid being defensive.

2. *Know what you want to bring out of the meeting before you go in.* This piece of self-instruction holds for any meeting, but is especially true for budget meetings. Avoid being sidetracked into nonessentials. Know where in your plans you will compromise, where you might consider a change, and where you will have to dig your heels in and fight any change.

3. *Keep the meeting moving.* When you are presenting your plans, you have the floor; use and keep it. If a question comes up, answer it and then move on to the next point. You want to avoid giving the impression that you are rushing through your plan and budget; but asking for questions, or even waiting to see if someone else has another question, is asking for trouble. One way in which you can show you have your responsibility center under control is to keep the meeting under control and moving. Rest assured that the person who will be approving your budget is not going to give his approval unless he is satisfied with your plans and proposed budget—and he will not be rushed. In both your manner and your words, you should assume agreement with and approval of your plans. A good way to fill a pause or move to the next point is the statement: "If there are no further questions, let's move on to the next point."

4. *Know when to pass the ball to your boss.* Because you have reviewed your budget and plan proposal with your boss (and perhaps even rehearsed your presentation with him), there will be no surprises for him in what you say at the meeting. But you may be surprised by one of the questions directed toward you. Make a stab at answering it; then if you feel that more should be said, but you're not sure exactly what, toss the question on to your boss. Sometimes just a pointed look at him will get him to say something that will resolve the matter and get you off the hook. When he is through amplifying the answer to the question, pick up the reins of the meeting again and go on to the next point.

After budget approval

After your budget meeting, and after the meetings on all the responsibility centers in your department or division, the controller or his staff will need the individual budgets, as approved, for use throughout the coming year in the various management performance reports they will prepare.

You will know, from the published timetable, your deadline for turning your approved budget over to them. In some situations, you will need to do some work on the numbers before turning them in. That is, if changes to one of your plans were discussed and decided upon during the budget meeting, you'll have to make sure later on to revise all the applicable parts of your budget accordingly. ■

Chapter 7.

Carving monthly targets out of the annual budget

In some companies, budget proposals are based on yearly plans and annual totals—with no breakdown of the figures involved into smaller time periods. If this is the case in your company, after the meeting and the approval of your annual budget, you will have to break each annual total down into time periods corresponding to the number of times budget-performance reports will be issued during the year. Since performance reports are issued monthly in most companies, let's look at how total year figures can be broken down into months.

Year-to-year trends

Much earlier, we looked briefly at year-to-year *trends* in business activity as well as annual cycles. To recap, let's first look at a series of numbers from a budget proposal.

	Three Years Ago, Actual	*Two Years Ago, Actual*	*Last Year, Actual*	*This Year, Projected*	*Next Year, Proposed*
Units	58,880	69,480	83,375	100,000	120,000
% Change	+17.5	+18.0	+20.0	+19.9	+20.0

Leaving aside for the moment what the units are—thousands or millions, dollars or doughnuts, grams or tons, income or expense—the line of percentages shows a consistent pattern of increase that has stabilized over the last two years, and it is forecast to continue next year. This pattern is the trend of results, and it comes under intense scrutiny at budget time. If, instead of a 20 percent increase for next year, the manager proposes a budget figure that is significantly greater (say, 30 percent) or significantly smaller (say, 10 percent) than a continuation of the trend, he'll have to marshal some strong reasons why! Even with a proposed 20 percent increase, those reviewing and approving the budget will have some rather pointed questions to ask. They may, for example, ask the manager to put this trend for his individual center in perspective—by comparing it with the trend of other centers within the company and with external trends or indicators in the market, the industry, or the economy as a whole. The wise manager will do his homework to answer these questions before they are asked during the budget presentation.

Annual cycles

When breaking an approved total year budget down into months, the manager has to be concerned with another pattern of results: *the cycle.* With only rare exceptions, cycles of business are annual, following the calendar and seasonal weather change rather closely. Thus, the pattern of results will repeat every 12 months. Earlier, we examined a dramatic cycle of activity when we looked at greeting cards. There are very few (if any) products or services used so evenly throughout the year that the annual cycle would appear as a straight line on a graph.

The manager must be aware of these two types of patterns because he has a large measure of control over them; he can influence results to change both the trend and the cycle. For instance, sheets and pillowcases are used daily, but one of the yearly high points in sales of these items is the now traditional White Sale in January; a manager planned this once, put it into effect, and thus created a new cycle.

Noncyclical activity

In planning his center's monthly activity for the coming year, the manager must keep in mind the possibility of noncyclical activities. Such activities include the introduction of a new product, the changeover of production processes or machinery, the close-out of a product or process or inventory.

In some areas of activity, monthly budget breakdowns can be prepared very easily—by computer. Computerization saves a great deal of thought and work for individual managers and is an acceptable method—provided the bases upon which the computer will work are acceptable. Given proper programming, the computer will do an accurate job of factoring both trend and cycle into a monthly breakdown. Although it will be guided by history, it can't judge whether the historical pattern makes sense when projected into next year, and (without special programming) it won't take into account either recent decisions designed to change the monthly pattern or any special, nonrepetitive activity planned for the coming year.

Monthly breakdowns: bench marks of progress

One thing more the manager should keep in mind at this time is that when he submits his monthly breakdown to the finance department, he is submitting to management the checkpoints by which his progress and activity during the year will be measured. Certainly, the total budget figure for the year is still the most important target—but month after month during the coming year, his performance for each month and for the cumulative year-to-date time period will be reported, compared with the applicable budget, analyzed, and commented upon. The other inescapable fact is that during the course of the year, variances between performance figures and budget figures will occur. Further, except in very unusual circumstances, the budget is the budget; once submitted, it is not changed. So a variance that arises because of faulty budgeting becomes an albatross around the manager's neck; his only hope is to prevent a recurrence of the situation the next time around. Because a manager's budget is his plan expressed in numbers, an accusation of faulty budgeting is the same as an accusation of faulty planning—and a manager who cannot plan is not a manager.

The worksheet method of breaking down the budget

Let's turn from this gloomy possibility to look at a method of planning the breakdown of a yearly budget into months, a worksheet method that can help the manager both identify and handle (1) historical trends and cycles, (2) planned cyclical activities, and (3) a planned one-time activity. This method, a fairly thorough one, is especially useful for a responsibility center whose activity depends on the actions or reactions of the market place. It has been used in planning monthly budgets for consumer packaged goods that are mass-produced, nationally distributed, and nationally advertised—and it works. Because it is especially useful in the area of unit sales, we have developed an example around this activity. See Exhibit 23, pages 84 and 85.

Note that there are blanks on this worksheet exhibit, which lists unit sales by month and cumulatively through twelve months for each of the three previous fiscal years. It lists the current budget in the same format and in the next column ("This Year Actual") lists monthly sales for the year to date (through August). It is September, "budget preparation" time. That's what the blanks are for.

But before worrying about the blanks, let's look at the history. The line across the bottom identifies the change in total results from year to year—the *trend.*

Cast your eye down the right side of any of the columns and examine the figures in the percent column. Look just at the percentage that each month's sales represent of the total, and you'll see the way sales developed during that year; you'll note when they peaked and when they dropped off. Assuming that the reasons for purchasing this product repeat on a yearly basis, the pattern you have just detected is its *cycle.*

Now take any month and look at the percent figure for that month across the four completed columns. They are not the same, but they are close.

Now look at the cumulative percentages in March. Three years ago, sales for the first quarter were 25 percent of total year sales. But since then, this cumulative percentage for the first quarter jumped to 28 percent two years ago, dropped to 26 percent last year, and was budgeted to be 26 percent this year. A look across the June cumulative percentage line shows that over half the year's sales occur in the first six months. A look across the August cumulative percentage line shows another interesting fact: Three-quarters or more of the product's yearly sales are made in the first eight months. Further examination shows that the fourth quarter is weak for this product.

We have looked just at the percentages so far. Now let's look at some of the unit sales figures. A glance across some of the months will show how difficult it is to get quick comparisons from the raw figures—in contrast with the patterns of activity that jumped out at us from a glance at the percentages.

Projections for the balance of the year

Now let's get to work on projections for the remaining months in this year. (As we work out the figures, you may want to write them in on Exhibit 23. Or you may want to write them on a separate sheet of paper while referring to the exhibit.) At the end of August, last month, we were a shade under cumulative budget. But we had a good August, and now in September a look at the order situation promises a very good month; call it 10 million units. (Note that because the exhibit is set up in thousands, for convenience, you would write 10,000 —not 10,000,000—in the unit column for this September.) Standing orders through the balance of the year are healthy, and we're due to complete shipments in October to that big new account in the South. So let's project October at 5.8 million. That will bring the cumulative figure through October to 89,657,000. With sales of slightly less than budget for the last two-month period, we can reach a yearly total of 100 million units. That's a nice round figure and a bit over budget; let's use it.

With these numbers written down on the worksheet, we can now compare this year's projected total with last year's actual—and find that we will deliver a 19.9 percent increase over last year versus a budgeted increase of 19.3 percent. Now we quickly calculate the percentages for the months in the column for this year, write them in, and our "This Year Actual" column will appear as shown in Exhibit 24, page 86.

Looking back along the lines of monthly percentages for the months we've projected, we see that September two years ago was 10 percent and the year before was 9 percent; that looks all right. For the last three months of this year, we've projected percentages in a 6–5–5 pattern, which is just how sales occurred three years ago. The budget this year calls for a 5–5–6 pattern, which now looks off-target. The plan of getting more sales into the fourth quarter than was the case in the last two years now looks as though it will be met.

Now let's look at next year. We start by looking at the very bottom line on the first blank column—the blank space for the percent change. By how much will unit sales grow next year over this year? Here's where knowledge of the product, the competition, the market, and all associated elements come into play. For the purposes of this

Exhibit 23: Budget planning worksheet, Widget Corporation of America

PRODUCT: BLUE BLIVITS (0.5 oz.) ITEM: UNIT SALES (IN THOUSANDS)

		3 YEARS AGO ACTUAL		2 YEARS AGO ACTUAL		LAST YEAR ACTUAL	
		UNITS	% TOT.	UNITS	% TOT.	UNITS	% TOT.
JAN.	MO.	4,122	7.0	5,558	8.0	6,670	8.0
FEB.	MO.	5,299	9.0	6,948	10.0	7,504	9.0
	CUM.	9,421	16.0	12,506	18.0	14,174	17.0
MAR.	MO.	5,299	9.0	6,948	10.0	7,504	9.0
	CUM.	14,720	25.0	19,454	28.0	21,678	26.0
APR.	MO.	5,888	10.0	8,338	12.0	9,171	11.0
	CUM.	20,608	35.0	27,792	40.0	30,849	37.0
MAY	MO.	5,888	10.0	6,253	9.0	8,338	10.0
	CUM.	26,496	45.0	34,045	49.0	39,187	47.0
JUNE	MO.	5,299	9.0	6,253	9.0	8,337	10.0
	CUM.	31,795	54.0	40,298	58.0	47,524	57.0
JULY	MO.	5,888	10.0	7,643	11.0	10,005	12.0
	CUM.	37,683	64.0	47,941	69.0	57,529	69.0
AUG.	MO.	6,477	11.0	7,643	11.0	9,171	11.0
	CUM.	44,160	75.0	55,584	80.0	66,700	80.0
SEPT.	MO.	5,299	9.0	6,948	10.0	5,836	7.0
	CUM.	49,459	84.0	62,532	90.0	72,536	87.0
OCT.	MO.	3,533	6.0	2,779	4.0	3,335	4.0
	CUM.	52,992	90.0	65,311	94.0	75,871	91.0
NOV.	MO.	2,944	5.0	2,084	3.0	3,335	4.0
	CUM.	55,936	95.0	67,395	97.0	79,206	95.0
DEC.	MO.	2,944	5.0	2,085	3.0	4,169	5.0
	CUM.	58,880	100.0	69,480	100.0	83,375	100.0
% CHANGE		+17.5		+18.0		+20.0	

Prepared: September 19xx

THIS YEAR BUDGET		THIS YEAR ACTUAL		NEXT YEAR		NEXT YEAR	
UNITS	% TOT.	UNITS	% TOT.	UNITS	% TOT.	UNITS	% TOT.
6,965	7.0	6,040					
8,955	9.0	9,007					
15,920	16.0	15,047					
9,950	10.0	10,952					
25,870	26.0	25,999					
10,945	11.0	10,877					
36,815	37.0	36,876					
8,955	9.0	8,948					
45,770	46.0	45,824					
9,950	10.0	9,993					
55,720	56.0	55,817					
8,955	9.0	8,008					
64,675	65.0	63,825					
9,950	10.0	10,032					
74,625	75.0	73,857					
8,955	9.0						
83,580	84.0						
4,975	5.0						
88,555	89.0						
4,975	5.0						
93,530	94.0						
5,970	6.0						
99,500	100.0		100.0		100.0		100.0
+19.3							

Exhibit 24

		THIS YEAR ACTUAL UNITS	% TOT.
JAN.	MO.	6,040	6.0
FEB.	MO.	9,007	9.0
	CUM.	15,047	15.0
MAR.	MO.	10,952	11.0
	CUM.	25,999	26.0
APR.	MO.	10,877	11.0
	CUM.	36,876	37.0
MAY	MO.	8,948	9.0
	CUM.	45,824	46.0
JUNE	MO.	9,993	10.0
	CUM.	55,817	56.0
JULY	MO.	8,008	8.0
	CUM.	63,825	64.0
AUG.	MO.	10,032	10.0
	CUM.	73,857	74.0
SEPT.	MO.	10,000	10.0
	CUM.	83,857	84.0
OCT.	MO.	5,800	6.0
	CUM.	89,657	90.0
NOV.	MO.	5,170	5.0
	CUM.	94,827	95.0
DEC.	MO.	5,173	5.0
	CUM.	100,000	100.0
% CHANGE		+19.9	

Exhibit 25

		NEXT YEAR UNITS	% TOT.
JAN.	MO.	9,000	7.5
FEB.	MO.	10,800	9.0
	CUM.	19,800	16.5
MAR.	MO.	11,400	9.5
	CUM.	31,200	26.0
APR.	MO.	12,000	10.0
	CUM.	43,200	36.0
MAY	MO.	10,800	9.0
	CUM.	54,000	45.0
JUNE	MO.	12,000	10.0
	CUM.	66,000	55.0
JULY	MO.	12,000	10.0
	CUM.	78,000	65.0
AUG.	MO.	12,000	10.0
	CUM.	90,000	75.0
SEPT.	MO.	10,800	9.0
	CUM.	100,800	84.0
OCT.	MO.	7,200	6.0
	CUM.	108,000	90.0
NOV.	MO.	6,000	5.0
	CUM.	114,000	95.0
DEC.	MO.	6,000	5.0
	CUM.	120,000	100.0
% CHANGE		+20.0	

example, however, we're going to look just at history. Both this year and last, the yearly sales trend has been a 20 percent increase, so we'll use this figure. Then we move up one line—and since a 20 percent increase over this year's estimate of 100 million means that our unit budget for next year will be 120 million, we enter this figure.

Monthly breakdowns for next year

The next step—and the real reason for this type of worksheet—is to break this 120 million figure down into twelve monthly pieces, the monthly budgets. You'll remember that, much earlier, when we briefly discussed breaking a yearly budget of 120 zillion into twelve months, we pointed out that breaking it into twelfths—10 zillion a month—was incorrect. It's easy to see that this approach would be incorrect here, too: Dividing our current figure by 12 would work out to a monthly percentage of 8.3 every month, and a quick glance at our worksheet shows just how few months over the past few years were at the 8 percent level. We are faced with a cycle of sales over the year, with highs and lows that we must take into account.

Therefore, before putting in any units for any month next year, let's first complete the right side of the column—the percent figure for each month. We can start anywhere; at the top and work down, or with key months, or even with the cumulative percentages at key periods during the year. But let's be guided by the analysis we made when we first looked at the history and by our thinking as we estimated sales by month for the balance of this year.

Continuing the pattern

First, we remember our thoughts about the last quarter of this year. So let's start by saying we want to continue the same pattern next year. October, November, and December thus get a 6, 5, and 5 respectively in the appropriate monthly percent-of-total slot. By subtracting from 100 percent, we can then complete the cumulative percentage figures for November, then October, then September.

Now let's look at the first quarter. The cumulative percentage for March over the past few years has been around 26 percent. Let's use this number and then look at the individual months of January, February, and March. First, January: Last year and the year before, it was 8 percent. But this year it was 6 percent. We'd like to go to 8 percent again, but let's ease it a bit and put January down for 7.5 percent. Subtracting this from 26, we know that February and March combined must be 18.5 percent. February has been a 9 percent month for three of the last four times; let's put a 9.0 percent down for February. Then March has to be 9.5 percent—which looks reasonable and which will also mean a smoother pattern through the first quarter than was the case this year when the plant was almost caught short at the sharp increase in demand in March.

Let's look at the next quarter now. In our earlier analysis of historical patterns, we noted that the first half of the year was responsible for more than half of the total year's sales. But we think we'd like to continue the pattern of reducing this amount (a pattern easily detected by running your eye across the June cumulative percentage line). So let's put the figure of 55.0 percent down for next year's cumulative percentage at the half mark.

Again, subtraction tells us that with March cumulative at 26.0 percent, the months in the second quarter must total 29.0 percent—which could be two 10s and one 9. April? Yes, that's been a high month; let's give it a 10.0 percent. Then let's give May a 9.0 percent, and June the remaining 10.0 percent. Now we quickly fill in the cumulative percentage figures for April and May—and we can look at the third quarter.

The cumulative total through September is 84.0 percent; since it is 55.0 percent through June, subtraction tells us that the third quarter must be 29.0 percent. This suggests a 10–10–9 pattern; let's put these figures down for July, August, and September; upon entering the cumulative percentages for July and August, we've completed the percent column.

We can now multiply the unit total for the year (120,000) by the monthly percentage figures to derive the unit figure for each month; transferring these figures will complete the rest of the column for next year. Then we sit back to analyze what we've done and how it looks. (See Exhibit 25, page 86.)

As we look over this first attempt at breaking down next year's total unit budget of 120 million into months, we first compare the monthly unit figures entered for next year with what they were this year. Right away, the comparison for January brings a question to mind: We did roughly 6,000,000 this year; can we do 9 million—half again as much—next year? July shows the same possible problem—but July this year dropped 2 million from July last year, so perhaps the 12 million tentatively budgeted for next year is all right. Most of the unit figures for the other months versus the actuals for the same months this year show about a 20 percent increase (the growth factor budgeted for the total year), though not all (next September, for instance, is only 8 percent over this September).

Summing up this first look, we feel that we need to do something about January. Either we reduce the budget for January and spread what we take out over one or more other months—or we leave it at 9 million and schedule a promotion to consumers or to the trade designed to make January sales reach the budget figure.

Adjusting the monthly budget figures

Here is where the last column (Exhibit 23) comes in handy—it's for a second, adjusted try at defining next year's budget by month. Here is where the manager in real life can use his knowledge of the actual situation, market, regional variations, competitive activity, and so forth to factor in refinements to the first budget attempts. And if he's still not happy after his second try, he can keep on with further alternatives on a piece of scratch paper. He is, after all, using worksheets—once he has made a firm decision, he can enter his final budget-breakdown figures on the form provided by finance.

Preparing a worksheet like the one we've been discussing for your specific needs is a bit of a chore if done manually. It will mean copying out a series of numbers to reflect monthly results for previous years, this year's budget, and this year's results to date, and it will probably mean consulting more than one source document. Once the numbers are down, a whole series of percentages have to be calculated. If you cannot talk your EDP people into having a worksheet compiled and printed by computer (show them Exhibit 23 as a model), then we strongly recommend doing it by hand. The patterns and cycles of activity shown by the monthly percentages—both vertically during each of the years, and horizontally for each month across the years—will bring many interesting facts (and insights) to light about your responsibility center.

The "reach" in a budget

Every manager knows, when he goes into his annual budget meeting, that he will come out of this meeting with a commitment to reach a certain performance result over the following twelve-month period. He goes in with a budget proposal; he comes out with a budget that he is committed to deliver. Knowing this, most managers are human enough to go in with a budget proposal that leans toward the conservative side; that is, their figures reflect an allowance for the possibility that some part of the plans they've made won't work. Management also knows this; after all, those who review and approve the proposed budget were once operating managers themselves. The reviewers and approvers will thus go into budget meetings with the intention of identifying such conservatism and building more challenge (higher goals) into the manager's budget.

For the continued growth and success of the company, the manager's approved budget must not be overly conservative. That's why experienced management will make sure that there is some "reach" in the budget commitment they will accept from the manager. Let's say that a manager knows he can deliver 10 percent more next year even if a key plan doesn't work. If he proposes a budget for next year that is only 10 percent greater, he is hurting himself—by taking the challenge out of his job, by removing the need to strive and reach out for new ways, new plans, new techniques.

In the preceding example on monthly budget breakdowns, the manager came face to face with the "reach" built into his budgeted growth when he looked at the large target set for next January's sales. This challenge led to his consideration of a special promotion to reach the goal—and the mental process involved, the decision he made, and the work he undertakes to implement his decision will all help him grow and develop as a manager.

In these days of ever-increasing inflation, it must be remembered that the element of "reach" may be present in an approved budget for a profit center even if the commitment is to keep next year's profit contribution the same as this year's. It is even tougher for the manager to commit himself to the same *percentage* of contribution. To overcome rapidly rising costs, a consideration of unit sales increases and unit price increases is just the start of the challenge.

But the individual manager must remember one thing: When the budget meeting is over, he will emerge with a budget that he is committed to deliver. For all of the following year, that budget is *his* budget. If management boosted his proposed figure to unrealistic heights during the meeting, then the manager will be resentful and frustrated all year long—and he will probably stop trying to "make budget." But in the final analysis, this situation is the manager's fault —for not having defended his original figure strongly enough, for not having marshalled his facts and reasons to convince management during the meeting that not just "reach" but a miracle was called for in the target they wanted. This situation is one of the most difficult a manager can face, and there are no easy ways to solve it. The manager's aim must be to prevent this kind of confrontation through conscientious preparation before the meeting and a strong though flexible plan for presenting both his budget and the plans upon which the budget is based. ■

Chapter 8.

Hitting budget targets and protecting profits

Although it once seemed as though the budgeting process would never be finished, it was—and all the approved budgets and monthly breakdowns were given to the finance department. During the last month of the fiscal year, there was that last scurry to make sure the last month (and thus the whole year) ended with results on target—or, perhaps, a little over.

Now it's time to start another fiscal year, with the new budgets and goals that were set for the coming twelve-month period. It's time to put proposed new plans into effect in order to reach the new objectives. The activity of each responsibility center continues, and the finance department continues to register the progress of each. As monthly performance reports are issued, variances from budget start showing up.

Because budgets are prepared on a theoretical or ideal basis, the numbers in performance and variance reports are normally rounded off to the nearest thousand (or other large multiple) for the sake of simplicity. Actual results will rarely match the budgeted number. Depending on the individual company and responsibility center, variances of plus or minus 1 to 3 percent are normal;

they can be explained (if required) with a very brief comment—such as, for example, "only 21 work days this month."

Early action on variances

Yet when two or three months' reports are in, and all of them are 1 to 3 percent under (or over), then the beginning of a trend must be suspected—and an analysis of the why, where, and what conducted. Early identification and correction of a downtrend will save much grief later on. Similarly, early identification and exploitation of an uptrend will build momentum—and upward momentum builds profits very nicely.

Biologists use the term *feedback.* When a finger touches a hot stove, for example, heat-sensitive nerve endings transmit or "feed" this information "back" to the nerve center. The nerve center promptly evaluates the message and speeds a message to the muscles—whereupon the finger is rapidly pulled away from the stove. Biologists call this pattern of events a reflex. In budgeting, much valuable information feeds back from activity and performance reports; a good manager soon builds a reflex of promptly evaluating this information and acting on it as soon as necessary.

Information bearing upon responsibility centers may come from many sources: others in the company; outside clients or suppliers; articles in consumer, trade, and professional publications. Whatever information we receive from whatever source—our own activities (feedback) or the activities of others in our industry, the country at large, or overseas—we must evaluate the information for its potential impact on our plans, performance, or results. The key concern, of course, is to determine what action is advisable in light of the information received.

Unforeseen developments

In business, as in everyday life, the only constant is change; the only fact the manager can really count on is that things won't stay the same. In fortunate circumstances, most of the changes in the situation his center faces will be small ones. In such cases, he or she usually needs only to determine and stay aware of what has changed or is changing.

Of course, the manager has foreseen and planned for some of the changes encountered. Yet today the economic situation and business developments in the U. S: and around the world are changing at a faster rate than ever before. This in turn has given greater scope and opportunity to the mythical Mr. Murphy's two laws:

1. If something can go wrong, it will.
2. Something that has gone wrong will get worse.

Accordingly, the manager today may face a variety of unfortunate events and unforeseen developments. There may be labor strikes, material shortages, cost increases, currency devaluations, new government regulations or taxes, and an acceleration in the rate at which consumers switch to competitors' products or services—to name a few. Only rarely is an unforeseen market or economic development favorable—and when it is, the dramatic change it brings can also pose a problem for the manager. It may be the best kind of problem—"How can we produce enough to satisfy increased demand?"—but a problem it is, nevertheless.

A revised estimate of results

When one of these situations develops, a manager's budget and the plans established to meet it suddenly become of merely academic interest. The first thing he or she must do is to define the new situation and its ramifications, forecast the impact on the responsibility center, and make a revised estimate of results. Once this forecast is presented to and accepted by management, it becomes the new standard for results that the manager is committed to achieve. It may be called the revised estimate, projection, or forecast—but never the "new budget." For the entire fiscal year, the budget remains as originally approved.

If the revised commitment differs sharply from the original budget, the people in finance may issue a supplementary report comparing results with the new target figures. But they will continue to report on results versus the original budget.

The individual manager, of course, may find this practice neither enjoyable nor reasonable. It can become quite frustrating to see results continue to be compared with budget figures that have become meaningless because of an unforeseen, unfavorable development. But this practice emphasizes today's critical need for proper planning and such planning techniques as management by objectives.

Shorter budgeting cycles

Some companies, by virtue of the type of business they are in, have found that an annual budget and plan are regularly upset by unpredictable developments that arise over the year—so they have gone to a shorter budgeting period. Accordingly, such companies have established two or more budgeting cycles per year.

Book publishers on a yearly profit-planning cycle, for example, have found that although some of their new releases sell in predictable quantities, one or two others are so right for the market in subject matter and timing that they become "best sellers" and move three to ten times as fast as expected. Of course, the converse also holds: Some books expected to set new sales records languish unbought. Faced with this situation, some publishers have taken up the practice of budgeting twice a year for a six-month period of time. But whether a company budgets two or more times a year, its official books are still kept on the basis of a full twelve-month fiscal year.

Going through the full budgeting process twice a year has been called a system of "rolling budgets." The manager following this system often feels that he has just started putting an approved budget into effect when it's time to start budgeting all over again. From higher management's point of view, this kind of system helps ensure that managers won't shortchange the development or planning side of budgeting in terms of their time and effort. In the more usual—annual—planning cycles, strong pressure for results may tempt managers to give more time and attention to implementing the plan than to developing it.

Profit protection

In his book *Future Shock,* Alvin Toffler examined the increasing velocity of change in life today and the new pressures it has put on people. Change has also led to a variety of new pressures on businesses and corporations. Without making value judgments about the various changes in effect today, let's just say that consumerism, environmentalism, affirmative action, inflation, and recession can all have an impact on the profits of almost every manufacturing or service enterprise. The "good old days" with their "good old ways" are gone. Profits in general are shrinking, and even when they have remained at the same apparent level, inflation has eroded their real value.

Brand managers, department and division heads, and top management should all identify and understand the impact on their responsibility centers of developments that are affecting profits today or that could affect profits in the future. A manager can expect a hard time at his budget meeting if he proposes only a small budgeted sales increase because of a recessionary trend and at the same time requests higher expenditures to cover inflationary increases in material, labor, and marketing support. Today, more homework is needed; more than ever before, planning must be done in the area of profit protection.

One obvious way to protect profits is simply to raise prices to the level that will maintain income at the (real) accustomed level. But this solution today may be either impossible or counter-productive. Several factors can rule against raising prices: formal price-control programs, informal but real pressure from regulatory agencies or competitive companies, and consumer reluctance in a recessionary economy to pay more for the same product or service.

Value analysis

Some years ago, a technique was developed for increasing profits through an analysis of the components of all the costs incurred in an operation. This technique, which is highly recommended today, is called value analysis.

Value analysis involves the systematic examination of all the specifications, practices, and procedures followed in manufacturing and distributing a product or providing a service. The aim is to identify which parts of the process can be changed to reduce costs while maintaining the quality and value of the product or service. A value analysis meeting may be attended by managers from manufacturing, purchasing, R&D, marketing, and sales; in it, the "good old ways" are examined and dissected to see if there might be a better new way.

Here are some questions that come up in a value analysis meeting: How can manufacturing productivity be increased? What current requirements or procedures keep the machines from running faster or require extra labor? Is there any unused or underutilized plant capacity? Can the specified raw materials or packaging materials be changed to less costly ones without affecting the product's quality, appearance, or shelf life?

Often in such meetings, a question from one manager about another manager's operations opens up a fruitful area for potential cost savings. We have seen purchasing managers, for example, question the rigid specifications they have been given for key ingredients. Discussion has revealed that considerable savings involving no loss in product quality can be made by using ingredients of a "standard" rather than a "special" quality. We have seen simple changes in packaging eliminate production-line bottlenecks while improving product protection.

Mass-produced products are particularly ripe for value analysis. Half a penny or less saved in the cost of each unit, when multiplied by the large number produced each year, yields considerable profit improvement. Examples of profit-improvement moves identified through value analysis include packaging (in 24 units versus 20), shipping twice a month in containers instead of weekly in L.T.L. (less than truckload) lots, and using one less color in printing a package carton or label.

Another interesting example of what can come from value analysis is the decision to change the budget treatment of a part of manufacturing cost. In one value analysis session, it developed that manufacturing could save some money if marketing would agree to a less complex package. But marketing opposed this change in the belief that it was precisely the package format that had attracted the current strong product demand. A simpler package was then costed out. Although the change to the simpler package was not made, management decided that the price difference between the simple and the complex package was to be removed from manufacturing's cost-of-goods budget and placed in marketing's sales promotion budget. The brand's profit contribution remained unchanged, of course. But thereafter, the premium that marketing was paying for the complexity was highly visible and came under close attention at budget presentation time. Management decided that if contribution were to slip or if product demand were to stabilize, with market share at a plateau, then the package could be simplified—and the money thus released in the sales promotion budget could be used for other promotional activities or for profit protection.

The preceding example shows just how flexible responsibility accounting can be. What to the accountant was a commonplace packaging expense ended up being apportioned between the marketing and manufacturing budgets. The aim was to simplify the understanding—and thus the planning and control—of this part of the activity and its cost.

The last word

Of course, a whole series of rigid rules and accepted practices must be followed in bookkeeping for official tax purposes. But there are none in responsibility accounting—except for the overriding imperative: The budget and the performance comparisons based on it *must* measure what they are supposed to measure.

In the current reality of ever-accelerating change, the system behind any individual budget or report should be questioned. "That's the way it's always been done" can never be the answer to "Why is it done this way?"

Thanks to the widespread use of computers, it is almost always possible to get more data. But although managers may find it useful to have more information, their main focus should be on having more *meaning* in their budgets and performance comparisons.

The numbers in a budget are, after all, only the shorthand numerical expression of a plan. The numbers in the periodically issued performance reports are the numerical expression of the progress made toward the committed goal. Proper definition, understanding, and interpretation of these numbers are vital to managers at all levels.

Because a manager is responsible for his unit's activities, his key duties are to plan and to control. The management technique of budgeting defines this responsibility, highlights the plans made to carry it out, and measures the progress achieved. Understanding the why and the how of this highly flexible tool can make a good manager even better. Proving his command of budgeting to higher management is a sure sign that he is ready for greater responsibility. ■